Table of Contents

Introduction

In this manual your employees will learn the basics in your restaurant kitchen. It is very important that your kitchen staff learn and understand everything outlined in this restaurant kitchen manual. In so many cases, most cooks don't know time and temperature, food safety, shelf life dates, basic position training and etc. During the interview process, you may run into an application that appears to be awesome. The applicant will say what they think you want to hear, they talk the talk, but can they walk the walk.

After you conducted a reference check you can decide if the applicant is a good fit for your restaurant. The next step is kitchen training. Everyone goes through kitchen training, whether they are experienced or non-experienced. You truly don't know if that applicant is on the up and up on their experience.

Typically, experienced employees will learn faster than non-experienced employees and therefore will require less training days. Non-experienced employees will require more attention (TLC) and quite possibly extended training days.

Why is a well-trained employee beneficial to your restaurant?

1. Provides better customer service to your guest
2. Creates consistent menu items to the customers
3. Employees will get less frustrated because they are well trained
4. Your employees will stay employed longer which will cost you less in training new employees
5. A well trained employee will work proficiently; these employees will require less supervision.

The restaurant kitchen manual contains basic fundamental information for any restaurant. Knowledge is power and with that power it will allow you to have an awesome restaurant will well-trained employees.

Restaurant Kitchen Position Training

Why do cooks need to be thoroughly trained?

They need to know your menu inside and out and they need to know how to prepare each menu item consistently. Your customers visit your restaurant for great tasting food. These customers may have a favorite menu item in mind, if the item is not prepared correctly and consistently your customers will know it and may choose to visit your competition.

This manual is for restaurant kitchen staff members. Kitchen employees need to be trained and master every position in your restaurant. If there is a call out or if sales is more than expected, management needs to jump in and help reduce the stress in whatever position that is falling behind.

This manual will give you detailed information on how to train your employee's in operational excellence and WOW customer service.

Training is an Investment not an Expense. Many restaurant owners and managers look at training as an expense rather than an investment.

59% of restaurants fail in the first 3 years. 26% the first year, 19% fail the second year and 14% fail the 3rd year. These are very scary statistics, this leaves no room for error, do it right the first time.

Training is not just to survive, it is to maintain a balance in which you can excel and conquer!

Training has been a part of everyone's life throughout time. Years ago, a young teenage boy would begin his training with an experienced mentor who knew the business. Without the proper training we all would be lost and broke. Training your employees is one of the smartest moves you can make your business successful. If people are not trained, how would we expect them to know the job or to do it correctly?

If you are putting your money and time into your work, then you want to make that an investment and not a gamble. The businesses that are surviving must be doing something right. Do you really want to lose your money in a gamble by going into a business with no training or tools, or do you want to invest your money into something that will lead you to profits?

Many people invest and open a restaurant and don't have the knowledge to make it succeed. The goal of this book is to give you guidance and tools to be prosperous in your business.

I really don't think anyone wants to fail; most of us dream of becoming successful. You need to do more than just dream, you need to take your time and think it out and plan it correctly.

Introduction

I am about to tell you of my personal experience. It was a tough road for me and I really did not know what I wanted to do. My wife told me quite often that in 2012 we will have our own business. Every time she said that to me, all I could think was, 'How is that going to happen?' She also said that it has to be something you really want to do and sometimes that is so much a "part of you" that you don't even realize that other people don't have that gift.

I wondered what I could do. I did a lot of research and there was one consistent comment most people said, "Do what you love." My wife pointed out to me that everything I do and say is about the restaurant business. I often refer to our home pantry as "dry storage" or our refrigerator as a "walk-in." For me, it's the Restaurant Business and I have been in it for over 25 years.

I love the business, I love being around people and the challenges that every day brings. I know it like the back of my hand. I have always been a company man, I have been through several Kitchen Training courses, although most of my experience came from on the job experience.

I believe in doing the right thing and applying common sense. I was fortunate to have worked with really great people; I was trained the right way and stuck to it consistently every day.

In this Kitchen Training Manual I have developed ways to help you gain success in your business. If you are just starting a business or just thinking about it, this will definitely be beneficial for you.

This manual explains step-by-step instructions in training kitchen staff and job descriptions to guide you in training your employees.

This manual gives you an understanding of how a restaurant should operate. A successful restaurant takes a lot of dedication on everyone's part. Much of the success of the restaurant is upon the Owner or General Manager. This person is a key player and oversees everything.

Other key roles are the restaurant managers and supervisors who run the shifts from day to day. A thriving business will have well trained leaders who are consistent among each other. Visualize a chain with links, and each link is a workplace leader.

Now visualize that the chains run a machine, what happens when you twist a wrench into the chains when the machine is running; it is most likely going to stop. Just like the engine, if the management team is not consistently promoting the same things, then the chain will be twisted up or broken and everything stops.

Managers learn correct policies, procedures and how the different positions function and how to keep it going in the right direction. The Managers make sure everything they learned is consistently occurring from day to day. To ensure the system works the General Manager or the owner oversees the rest of the management.

Introduction

In addition, each crew member needs to be trained correctly. For the best results one or two certified trainers need to responsible for the training. If you are going to train someone and spend the money for it, then it is best to do right the first time. This manual will teach people, whether they possess experience or no experience in the food service industry. Easy to understand step by step instructions with clear understanding of all topics outlined in this manual. This is one of the most important positions to set the tone for the correct procedures that need to be installed in all employees.

In order for the training process to be effective the trainers need to be selected by the following criteria:

- Consistency in following all established policies and procedures.
- Mature in age and in doing the right thing for the right reasons.
- Takes criticism well and uses it toward correcting the issue.
- Respects all other employees, including the management team.
- Does not follow the crowd, but sticks to what is correct.
- Position knowledge and execution above standard.
- Has the best interest of the restaurant in mind.
- Has a passion for keeping the business profitable.
- Knows the importance of high quality customer service.

It is recommended to promote this person into the position as trainer if possible. If you do not have a certified trainer, then it is recommended to use a manager with the qualities noted above. You cannot afford to let a non-qualified trainer train your employees. I have been in the business for years and I have seen inadequate training occur in over 75% in the cases.

The worst thing you can do is to let an inexperienced or poorly trained employee train a new person. In my experience, it is an unfortunate event that often occurs; an employee with bad habits or poor training teaches incorrect information to the new staff members. Training is very costly, and you cannot afford to keep hiring, training and losing employees.

This is a domino effect-the non-qualified employee trained someone incorrectly, and the bad habits continue to be passed on as new staff come in. The new person who is poorly trained gets frustrated and either quit or continues the incorrect behavior. This is often referred to as a "rotating door."

As a tool to help you keep the restaurant in the above average area I would encourage you to empower the trainers to be able to correct any employee that are not following procedures or policies whether they are training or not training.

Think of it as a second pair of eyes. To take it further, invite them to participate in the manager meetings. This gives the trainers a strong sense of support and they know their job is an important role in the team. The trainers can give excellent input on issues that may be occurring in the restaurant.

Consistency is the Key to your Restaurant's Success

It has been said time and time again that consistency creates success. But if it's really as easy as it sounds, why aren't all restaurant owners wildly successful?

Think back to a time in your life when you achieved some form of success – whether it was in academics, in sports or in business. Maybe you aced a big exam, winning a particular trophy, or exceeding a sales target.

In the time leading up to that successful moment, you most likely made an intentional decision to commit yourself to achieving that goal. Perhaps you studied every day for a week before the exam. Or regularly trained with your team before the big game. You were determined to remain consistently persistent and do whatever it took to win.

So what's stopping you from applying that same diligence and determination into your daily routine today?

The information that was gathered to create this manual was from individuals that worked in the restaurant industry, specifically corporate restaurants for over 25 years.

"It's not what we do once in a while that shapes our lives, but what we do consistently."
Tony Robbins

"We are what we repeatedly do. Excellence, then, is not an act, but a habit."
Aristotle

Before any employee is hired it might be a really great idea to do a thorough background check, job reference check, personal finances check and drug test.

Before you hire any employee you should do a thorough previous job reference check. Do the interview first, and then do a job reference check. When doing a reference check match up the reference check to the application and interview for consistent information.

If you do not do a reference check on your employees, you are risking everything. Do you know who you are hiring? The last thing you need is an employee who is dishonest and non-performing. This will also create a rotating door of employees who are either terminated or an employee who quit.

This route can be very expensive, it is best to do the right thing and do the reference check to avoid the loss of time and money.

Before the first day of training begins, the paperwork and orientation must be completed.

Paperwork consists of the following

- Completely filled out Job application.
- W-4: Go to this website to print out a W-4 www.irs.gov/pub/irs-pdf/fw4.pdf
- I-9: Go to this website to print out a I-9 www.uscis.gov/files/form/i-9.pdf
- Work permits (See the below pages for PA minor laws).

   __Always refer to your own State laws regarding paperwork, minor laws and wages.__

On the next page are topics to go over with your employees. These Orientation topics are more common in most restaurants.

Orientation
Orientation Topics and Information

The Instructor's Background

Use this time to introduce yourself as the class instructor. Discuss your background with the Restaurant or in the restaurant industry.

Employees at the Restaurant

Identify the following leaders in the Restaurant Organization. Explain their role in the success of the Restaurant (or provide an opportunity for them to introduce themselves).

- Restaurant owner
- Area supervisor
- General manager
- Restaurant chef
- Assistant manager
- Front of house manager
- Back of the house manager
- Lead cook
- First cook
- Shift leader
- Certified trainers

History of the Restaurant

Start off with the name of the business and who owns it and where the restaurant is located in (what state)? Describe the restaurant concept (Uniqueness).

The Restaurant has created success by:

Examples are:

- Using the highest quality chicken, shrimp, and beef for all dishes.
- Accepting only friendly service and high quality food.
- Focusing on quick serve and take out business.
- Focusing on guest satisfaction, team building, and product excellence to lead the industry.

What is The Restaurant?

The Restaurant concept has always focused on serving fresh, high quality food, cooked to order and served in a friendly, exciting, and clean environment. All products used or sold in our restaurants are ordered from the Company's centralized warehouse. This centralized distribution helps us control product quality and consistency.

Mission:
To Be Exceptional with the Essentials
- Guest excellence
- Great tasting food
- Sparkling clean restaurants
- Positive profit line

Our Vision: Be Extraordinary with the Essentials

Our Credo: WOW each guest, each and every time; no excuses, no exceptions!

What it takes:
- **Integrity-** Be honest; hold yourself accountable for your actions.
- **Zeal to serve-** Going beyond the basics, desire to help others.
- **Excellence-** an attitude or feeling to strive for perfection, to do the best.
- **Teamwork-** everyone working towards a common goal and mutual respect for everyone's abilities.
- **Truthful communication-** Be specific with information. Set clear expectations.

Did You Receive…? Ask if team members have received the following items. Be prepared to explain all items. Distribute any missing items.
- **Job description:** Describes employee responsibilities and requirements for each job.
- **Menu description:** Describes and lists ingredients for each menu item.
- **Employee handbook:** Outlines employee benefits/laws, responsibilities, and Company information.
- **Restaurant training material:** Includes handouts and training guides.
- **Training agenda:** Schedules and training topics.

Breaks/Conditions/Teens:
Employers are responsible for providing employees with periodic breaks in a cool area, with fans or air conditioning, ventilation and cold beverages. The potential for heat stress is heightened for kitchen workers due to steam, hot grills and stoves.

Restaurant employees should be educated on the dangers and symptoms of heat stress, such as dehydration, exhaustion, fainting and heat stroke. Teenagers employed in the restaurant are only permitted to work limited hours until the age of 18. Children under 16 years of age are banned from baking or cooking, and using devices that may cause injury, such as stoves, knives and grills. Refer to your state for information regarding breaks and conditions.

Minor Breaks
Teen workers (under age 18) are entitled to an uninterrupted meal break of at least 30 minutes if they work more than 5 hours in a day. They also are entitled to at least a 10-minute paid rest break for each 4 hours worked. They must be allowed a rest period no later than the end of the third hour of the shift.

Orientation
Orientation Topics and Information

Regulations Breaks

Every employee is permitted (as far as practical) a rest period during each work period. The authorized rest period is based on the total hours worked daily. For every four hours of work time, every employee is allotted one ten-minute rest time. (Example, 2 breaks in an 8-hour shift, 1 break in a 4-hour shift) Team members who work less than 3.5 hours are not allotted a rest period.

Meals

- Team members who work more than 6 hours during a shift receive a minimum of 30 minute mealtime without pay.
- Team members who work less than 6 hours during a shift are not entitled to a 30-minute mealtime and can eat before or after signing in or during the allotted 10-minute rest period.
- Team members are eligible to enjoy items from the employee menu during each work shift.
- Team members can eat on schedule breaks or order takeout before clocking out.
- 6 hours or less entitled to a lunch employee meal (50% discount) excluding shrimp and white chicken dishes.
- 6 hours or more entitled to a lunch employee meal (free) excluding shrimp and white chicken dishes.

Conduct Off-Duty
Team members must adhere to the following guidelines when off duty:

- Team members are not permitted in the BOH or checkout areas.
- When entering the restaurant during business hours, team members must comply with the dress code and rules of conduct in front of our Guests.
- Team members must enter and leave through the front door only
- Team members are always welcome to enjoy our restaurant as a Guest. We simply ask that they comply with the standards of behavior and dress that we ask of our Guests. Also, the rules of conduct for on-duty team members apply to off-duty team members while on the premises. The employee's presence reflects on the restaurant and other team members who work for the Company.

Smoking

Smoking by team members is prohibited in the restaurant and food preparation areas. (Communicate the team members' designated smoking area at the restaurant). Remove all cigarette butts and debris from this area before returning to work from a "smoke-break." Note: Smokers do not receive extra breaks because they smoke.

Company Phone

Family members can call the restaurant main phone only in the event of an emergency. Employees are prohibited from using the restaurant house phone; this phone is reserved for restaurant business only. However, if you ask permission to use the phone the manager may be inclined to let you use the phone for local calls only.

Orientation
Orientation Topics and Information

Scheduling Postings
For example: Work schedules are posted by Thursday of each week. See your general manager for your restaurant's schedule posting.

Shift Switching
Permissible: only with authorization from the manager.

Overtime
Based on state laws overtime can be paid (time and a half) for every hour over 8 hours worked during a day or every hour over 40 hours worked during a week.

Calling Out
You are required to call at least 3 hours ahead of time if you know you are going to miss a shift. When possible, try to cover your own shift before making the phone call to your Manager.

Tardiness
Other team members, as well as your manager and our guests are depending on your prompt attendance to work. The restaurant does not tolerate tardiness. However, if you know you are going to be late, phone in and let the manager know as quickly as possible so arrangements can be made to cover that time. Continued tardiness can result in termination of employment from the restaurant.

Evaluation and Wages
Hiring wages are based on current experience in the restaurant industry. However, The restaurant recognizes excellent performance through increased salary.

Wage Increases
Over time, you can increase your earnings by demonstrating professionalism in the following areas:

- **Experience:** Starting wages depend on your experience in the restaurant industry.
- **Attitude:** A positive, "can-do" attitude with the desire to learn new skills and help team members accomplish the tasks required to complete a shift.
- **Consistent Performance:** Professional performance in your station, all team members are required to perform above standard.
- **Evaluation Ratings:** Evaluations provide a means of identifying areas of success and improvement for team members. All team members are provided the opportunity to complete an employee evaluation with their supervisor. Merit increases are reliant on above-average evaluations.

Evaluations:

Quarterly for Back of House Staff

Quarterly evaluations should be done for Kitchen/BOH staff. Because of the intensity and pace in the kitchen, you may also have quick reviews of performance on a monthly basis to make sure skills and performance are at the restaurant standard.

Pay Periods

Checks are available on a regular basis depending on the payday policies. Be respectful of peak business hours when picking up paychecks. Best times 2-4 pm.

POS Time Keeping

Team members use the Point of Sale system to clock in and out. Conduct a training session for this procedure. Make sure team members know to immediately report any discrepancies in time to the Manager on Duty. Team members are charged for the replacement of lost or stolen cards, If applicable.

Pay and Benefits / Pay depends on experience

Remind all management and staff that they should not discuss their pay with another team member. That is private information designed for that employee based on experience, knowledge, education and training. Benefits will be explained by the General Manager on an individual basis.

At will employment

At will employment describes the employment relationship between employers and employees in almost every state.

At will employment means that the company does not offer tenured or guaranteed employment for any period of time to any employee without an employment contract or written direction from the CEO/President.

In at will employment either the company or the employee can terminate the employment relationship at any time, with or without cause, with or without notice.

Harassment

The Restaurant supports a no tolerance policy for harassment based on race, sex, religion, disabilities, or gender preference. No tolerance means the offender will automatically be investigated and possibly disciplined or terminated for any harassment allegations brought against him/her.

Parking

Most restaurants do not allow staff members to park in prime parking spaces. These areas are reserved for restaurant customers only. The owner of the restaurant will ultimately decide where staff members will park their vehicles while they are on duty. Make sure you park in a lighted area for safety. You can be fined for parking in handicapped spaces.

Dress Code, Uniform

The Restaurant requires every employee to wear a uniform (described below) while on the clock. As an employee of The Restaurant, you are our representative to the Guest. Uniforms help Guests easily identify team members who can help them. Uniforms are also designed for maximum safety while working.

The following uniform standards apply to every employee while:

- Working in the restaurant.
- Catering on location.
- Completing marketing assignments (delivering door hangers, etc.).

While wearing your uniform, especially when you are off the property or off the clock you are expected to act professional because you still represent the restaurant and the owner.

Grooming and Hygiene

Communicate the following grooming standards to team members:
- Hair clean and combed.
- Hair must be confined (a bun or up under a hat). If hair is in a ponytail and it hangs at shoulder length or longer, confine it further in a braid etc.)
- Hair color must be a natural color (not the color of the rainbow) unless the company specifies differently.
- Employees must be clean shaven. Goatees are allowed (If applicable) as long as they are kept neat and trimmed side's burns may not exceed mid-ear length. See management for facial hair guidelines.
- Fingernails trimmed and clean. Fake nails are not to be worn; nail polish will be neutral in color.
- Employees are expected to be clean, without excessive body odors or perfumes.
- Tattoos are to be covered up, by using Band-Aids or long sleeve shirts unless the company specifies differently.

Orientation
Employee Uniform Policies

The following items are provided by the restaurant.
See your hiring manager for your uniform requirements, every restaurant is different.

Back of the House
Name Tag (BOH): If applicable

Full Time
_____ Shirts/Polos - shirt tucked into pants: If applicable
_____ Hat: If applicable

Black pants, jeans or corduroys: If applicable
An apron • Full apron provided by the restaurant: If applicable

_____

Back of the House
Name Tag (BOH). If applicable

Part Time
_____ Shirts/Polos - shirt tucked into pants: If applicable
_____ Hat: If applicable

Black pants, jeans or corduroys: If applicable
An apron • Full apron provided by the restaurant: If applicable

_____

The following will be provided by the Employee.
See the hiring manager for work shoes purchase policy. If applicable

Oil/slip Resistant Shoes
Wal-Mart or Kmart provides a special selection of non-slip shoes work and steel-toe shoes.

Safety is everyone's responsibility.

No one should ever open the back door at night. The reason for keeping the door closed is primarily for security reasons because of robberies.

In today's society, especially in today's economy, unfortunately robbery is a very common occurrence. You read about robberies in the newspaper, on the news and on TV. Businesses get robbed and people even get killed.

Most companies have very stiff policies about going out the back door at night; in fact, in a lot of companies they will terminate you if you have opened the back door at night, or if you prop the door open at any time. If a robbery occurs, it is important that you NEVER fight back. It only makes things worse. The safest thing to do is to cooperate and give them what they want. It is not worth putting yourself, your coworkers or customers lives in danger.

The best thing you can do is to be very observant

- How many people were involved?
- Could you tell if they were male or female?
- How tall was he/she?
- Hair color / eye color / skin color?
- What kind of clothes are being worn?
- Any visible marks on the robbers, such as – tattoos or cuts.
- Do any of the robbers have accents or speech impairments
- Did you see any vehicle when they arrived or left? Get the license number and the make/model, if possible.

Always enter the restaurant with two employees, at least one should be a manager, and usually the second is a cook or server. When the manager opens the door, a walk through needs to be conducted looking for anyone that might be hiding.

When closing the restaurant nightly, always lock the door for security reasons after the last customer leaves the restaurant.

When counting money never count in view of the guest, once the money is counted it need to be secured in a lock box or the safe in the office.

In some companies it is required for the employee to sign a policy/procedure agreement. This provides some sort of paper trail.

It is the owners and management's responsibility to promote a non-sexual harassment atmosphere. Managers or supervisors must not allow any type of sexual harassment to occur in the workplace. If sexual harassment occurs and the manager did nothing to fix it, then the manager is equally guilty and could be held accountable. If an employee files a lawsuit in regards to sexual harassment, then you are putting the restaurant in jeopardy. One single lawsuit will make a huge dent in your bottom line. Do you really want to take that chance?

What is Quid Pro Quo?

The Latin term quid pro quo translates to **"something for something."**

Therefore, quid pro quo harassment occurs in the workplace when a manager or other authority figure offers are merely hints that he or she will give the employee something (a raise or a promotion) in return for that employee satisfaction of a sexual demand. This also occurs when a manager or other authority figure says he or she will not fire or reprimand an employee in exchange for some type of sexual favor. A job applicant also may be the subject of this kind of harassment if the hiring decision was based on the acceptance or rejection of sexual advances.

For instance, a male bank manager interviewing a female applicant for a job as a teller places his hand on her thigh. When she objects, he asks, "Don't you want this job?" The implication is that she must comply with the hiring manager's advances in order to get hired.

Learn what sexual harassment is and how to prevent it in the workplace.

http://www.nolo.com/legal-encyclopedia/preventing-sexual-harassment-workplace-29851.html

It is unlawful to harass a person (an applicant or employee) because of that person's sex. Harassment can include "sexual harassment" or unwelcome sexual advances, requests for sexual favors, and other verbal or physical harassment of a sexual nature.

Harassment does not have to be of a sexual nature, however, and can include offensive remarks about a person's sex. For example, it is illegal to harass a woman by making offensive comments about women in general. Both victim and the harasser can be either a woman or a man, and the victim and harasser can be the same sex.

Although the law doesn't prohibit simple teasing, offhand comments, or isolated incidents that are not very serious, harassment is illegal when it is so frequent or severe that it creates a hostile or offensive work environment or when it results in an adverse employment decision (such as the victim being fired or demoted). The harasser can be the victim's supervisor, a supervisor in another area, a co-worker, or someone who is not an employee of the employer, such as a client or customer. Sexual harassment in the workplace can be very costly for the restaurant if you are in a lawsuit. Protect your assets and create a non-sexual harassment workplace.

Orientation
Open Door Policy

Businesses that wish to foster an environment of cooperation and respect between the senior management team and employees creates open door policies. This policy leads to greater communication between managers and employees, but the policy must be monitored carefully to ensure the spirit in which it was created is not abused or compromised.

An open door policy allows employees to bypass their immediate supervisors and seek out senior managers to discuss job and personal issues. Much of the time, the issue is something the employee does not feel comfortable discussing with his immediate supervisor or his immediate supervisor is part of the issue.

With an open door policy, employees can approach senior management and discuss issues such as job performance, conflicts with co-workers, ideas for department improvements and company policies.

Open door policies foster communication between employees and management. The policy offers an alternative discussion forum for employees with supervisors who lack managerial skills or are prone to acts of intimidation.

The problem-solving skills of the management team also improve with such a policy; senior management encourages the employee to approach his immediate supervisor and also provides guidance to middle management for discovering managerial issues.

The policy creates an environment of trust between the employees and management. When an employee understands that he has someone to go to when his immediate supervisor is not an option, his trust in the company grows.

Open door policies can lead to employees automatically going over their immediate supervisor's heads for every issue. Bypassing immediate supervisors rob those supervisors of the ability to solve problems they normally would handle.

It also leads to tension between employees and middle management. Consistent bypassing might cause the manager to suspect the employee of undermining him in an attempt to cause problems between him and senior management.

A business opting to institute an open door policy must be specific about rules put into place regarding its use. For example, an employee must attempt to discuss the issue with his immediate supervisor before involving a senior manager. It also must be clear that with the exception of obvious immediate supervisor malfeasance, the open door policy is not **a form of discipline for the immediate supervisor.**

The responsibility of ensuring that the proper channels are followed falls to senior management.

For example, if the issue is with that particular shift manager and the employee does not feel comfortable in discussing that issue with that manager, then the employee may use the open door policy chain of command. Make an appointment to speak to the general manager to voice your concerns. If the issue is still not resolved, then the next step is to go up the chain of command and speak to the owner or district manager.

If the problem still persists, keep moving up the chain of command until you are satisfied and the problem has been fixed. If you utilize the open door chain of command procedure, the employee should not be in fear of appraisal from any manager or other employee.

If this occurs, then immediately report that manager or staff member to the owner, general manager, district manager or human resources department. Remember the open door policy; follow the chain of command in order.

The minimum age for employment is 14 years old unless you are employed on a farm or domestic service, and then there are no restrictions.

Permits are required for all jobs except farm work:

- 12 years old to be a caddy at a golf course.
- You must be at least 11 years old to deliver newspapers.
- 7 years old for theater, modeling and television.
- No restrictions on the motion pictures.

Everyone less than 18 years of age needs an employment certificate (working papers) unless you are 17 and graduated or officially terminated from school.

There are three types of employment certificates in many states for Minors:

- General employment certificate: For any minor no longer enrolled in school.
- Vacation employment certificate: For any minor still enrolled in school.
- Transferable employment certificate: For 16 or 17 year old minors. Can usually be transferred between employers. (Optional)

NOTE: Working papers are generally issued at the school where the child is enrolled.
Teenagers employed in the restaurant are only permitted to work limited hours until the age of 18. Children under 16 years of age are banned from baking or cooking, and using devices that may cause injury, such as stoves, knives and grills. Refer to your state for information regarding breaks and conditions.

Working papers are usually issued at the school where the child is enrolled.

Minor Breaks
Teen workers (under age 18) are entitled to an uninterrupted meal break of at least 30 minutes if they work more than 5 hours in a day. They also are entitled to at least a 10-minute paid rest break for each 4 hours worked. They must be allowed a rest period no later than the end of the third hour of the shift.

Overview of the minor hours of work (based on US regulations as of July 2016)
During the School year

14 and 15 year olds:

- Are not permitted to work more than **4 hours per day** and
cannot work before 7 am or after 7 pm during the school year.

16 and 17 year olds:

- Not more than 8 hours per day and 28 hours per school week.
- Cannot work before 6 am or after 12 am (midnight) on school days before 6 am and 1 am on Fridays and Saturdays.

Summer time

During the summer time 14- 15 year olds are permitted a maximum of 8 hours per day and up to 10 pm.

There are no starting and stopping hour restrictions on what can be worked during the summer vacation, but at no time can a minor work more than 8 hours per day or 44 hours per week.

Penalties

There can be significant penalties for violating the Child Labor Law. Any person, including agents and managers, who violates the Child Labor Law can be sentenced to pay a fine for a first offense of between $200.00 and $400.00, and, on a subsequent offense, to pay a fine of between $750.00 and $1,500.00, or to undergo an imprisonment of not more than ten days, or both, at the discretion of the court.

The Pennsylvania Code also sets out specific penalties for violating individual Code sections, which can carry misdemeanor penalties. Refer to your state child laws for pertinent information regarding minors in your state.

In most cases the work permit is issued by the school where the child is attending. Instruct the minor to go to their school to obtain the application and then bring it back to the restaurant. The Manager or General Manager needs to fill out the form and then sign it.

Once the work permit is issued the minor needs to bring it back to the restaurant and a copy is made and that that copy is placed in the minor's employment file. The original work permit always stays with the minor.

You cannot let a minor work at any establishment without a validated work permit. Once again, please refer to your state laws as it is different from state to state.

Check your state, age requirements as it may be different from state to state

Check your state, age requirements as it may be different from state to state

Some prohibited occupations are:

- Bowling centers (except snack bar attendant, control desk clerk and scorer)
- Building heavy work
- Highway (open road)
- Where liquor is sold or dispensed
- Manufacturing
- Scaffolds and ladders
- Window cleaning (above ground)

These were just some examples of prohibited occupations under Pennsylvania's Child Labor Law. For more details on these and other occupations or any other information on the Child Labor Law, go online to http://www.dli.state.pa.us/ and click on Labor Laws or 1-800-932-0665

There may be additional restrictions placed on minors by the Federal Government.

You can find out more on their web site or by calling;
http://www.youthrules.dol.gov/Default.html
Call 1-866-4-USWAGE

Minor Laws are maybe different from state to state –

Please refer to your state laws so you can stay within the law.

OSHA Training

The Restaurant is committed to a safe work environment and partners with the Occupational Safety and Health Administration (OSHA) to ensure each employee is trained and understands their responsibilities in maintaining a safe and healthy work environment. The OSHA Training provided by the restaurant outlines the practices for a safe environment.

OSHA Regulations for Restaurants

The United States Department of Labor Occupational Safety and Health Administration (OSHA) require that employers follow safety regulations to ensure the health of their employees.

Restaurant employees are protected under OSHA rules from poor conditions and hazards that may cause potential work-related injuries or fatalities. Establishments are inspected regularly to guarantee that employers are in compliance with OSHA guidelines.

Surface Maintenance

OSHA restaurant regulations include the maintenance of floors, aisles and walkways within all areas of the restaurant. OSHA law requires that passageways, storage rooms, kitchen areas, dining rooms, restrooms and bar areas are kept clean and dry.

Dishwashing stations or bar areas that are prone to water build-up should be provided with drainage, mats, false floors or platforms to prevent slipping or falling and related injuries. Floors must be free of protrusions, such as nails, and hazards, including loose boards, splinters and holes.

Aisles and passageways must be clear of obstructions and should be marked. Guardrails are required for stairs, steps, platforms and ramps.

Fire Safety

Restaurants need to supply portable fire extinguishers to protect employees in case of fire. Employers must inspect, maintain and test fire extinguishers. Maintenance is effective in ensuring the devices are fully charged and working.

Employers are required to provide a certification record signed and dated by the person who administered the fire extinguisher tests at the indicated time intervals required. Fire extinguishers should be stored in designated spots within the restaurant. Employers are responsible for alerting restaurant employees to where the fire extinguishers are located and informing them of a safety plan in place.

National Restaurant Association Educational Foundation
2055 L St. NW
Washington, DC 20036
Phone: 800.424.5156
Website: www.nraef.org

Pennsylvania Restaurant & Lodging Association
Their normal business hours are Monday through Friday, 8:30 AM. To 5:00 PM.
100 State Street
Harrisburg, PA 17101
Phone: (717) 232-4433 | (800) 345-5353
Fax: (717) 236-1202

Email: info@prla.org
Website: http://www.prla.org/

Certification Information
One certified food protection manager required per facility and accessible at all times during facility operation hours.

Serve Safe Certification Renewal Every 5 years.

New employees will have 90 days from starting employment to become certified. The online exam is now approved for use in the state. For additional information, contact PA Department of Agriculture.

All the above are Pennsylvania regulations – **Go to the National website to get more information on your state regulations:** http://www.nrfsp.com/en/State%20Regulations.aspx

Restaurant Kitchen Training

Effective Restaurant Kitchen Training 101

26

Restaurant Kitchen Position Training

Why does the manager need to be trained in as a cook?

Realistically, you can't close the restaurant if your employees call out, especially if that employee is a cook. Do you have any idea how much money you will lose if that manager were to close the restaurant? Your managers need to be fully trained in the kitchen in case of a call out or if sales are higher than expected.

The managers or supervisors should frequently verify that the kitchen customer checks hanging on the rail in the kitchen area with-in the standard check times. If the customer checks are not with-in the standard check times below, then the manager needs to help the kitchen cook until the checks are within the standard check times.

If the manager cannot leave the kitchen, then the server should talk to their guest and if necessary give them a complimentary cup of soup or side salad until the issue has been resolved. You should only do this if the check is 25 to 30+ minutes off. You should be able to read your guest body language to determine if they are okay or not okay.

The manager should talk to the customers that were affected and make sure that they are okay, if not with-in reason fix the issue.

Breakfast	8 Minutes or less
Lunch	10 Minutes or less
Dinner	15 minutes or less
Appetizers	7 Minutes or less
Soups, Salads and Sodas	4 Minutes or less

Once the manager is fully trained, then they can monitor and correct employees in different positions. The manager needs to be held at a higher standard than the staff members. Also, the manager needs to master each position not just know it, live it.

Kitchen Training
Opening Kitchen Responsibilities

The opening manager or opening cook should turn on the lighting and the hood fans in the kitchen first thing in the morning. Stagger on all kitchen equipment; only use what the business calls for. Turn on equipment at least 30 minutes before use.

Make sure the grills have been cleaned thoroughly and seasoned.

How to properly season a grill

While surface is slightly warm, spread oil using a cloth or paper towel. Turn heat back on to 350. Heat until oil on the griddle begins to smoke, then turn off and allow to cool. After cooling, wipe up any excess oil.

Set up a sanitation bucket with the proper level of sanitation liquid in it.

Quaternary Ammonia

Quaternary ammonium Sanitizers (Quat) are great for sanitizing kitchen walls, floors and countertops. They are much less corrosive than chlorine and iodine Sanitizers, so the chances of damage to surfaces are minimal. Quaternary Ammonia will properly sanitize stainless steel prep tables, the inside of commercial refrigerators, shelving, and other surfaces.

Quaternary Ammonium Sanitizer mixtures should be concentrated between 150 ppm and 400 ppm in 75-120 degree water. Like the other sanitizers, be sure to read the manufacturer's label and mix according to their directions and the health code regulations in your area. Quaternary Ammonium are easily dispensable from a wall mount above your three-compartment sink, whereas chlorine and iodine are not as easily dispensed. Always use test strips to determine if the sani water is at the right sanitation level. Change the water every 4 hours or as needed.

Set up all utensils, spatulas, grill scrapers, tongs and ladles. Make sure you have enough plates to get through the peak period. Stock all carryout containers, soufflé cups / lids and soup cups.

Check the stocking levels in the entire kitchen - refrigerator and freezer units. Check for expired date dots. Also make sure all products is rotated properly (FIFO). Make sure every employee working specific positions understand your expeditions and goals for the shift, talk them into position.

Every employee will be assigned a specific cleaning task & side work assessments. These assignments & cleaning task should be completed before the end of their shift. A manager needs to verify that the cleaning task and side work has been completed before the employee goes home for the day or night.

I recommend writing down the cleaning task and side work on an index card. When the employee arrives to work give them the card with the information on it, communicate your expeditions and time goals. Tell the employee the cleaning task and side work must be completed before the scheduled shift is done and that you must verify that the work has been completed.

Employees must meet the standard check times during the shifts and should apply sense of urgency.

*Note any previous night's closing issues, communicate those issues to management

As the closing employees arrive to work the kitchen should be turned over to them in the same shape that the opening employees receive it. Each shift sets up the next shift up for success.

The closing employees before the peak time period begins should completely stock the kitchen. Do not over stock as this will create unnecessary waste. Stock just enough to get through the shift without running out.

Set up a sanitation bucket with the proper level of sanitation liquid in it.

Quaternary Ammonia

Quaternary ammonium Sanitizers (Quat) are great for sanitizing kitchen walls, floors and countertops. They are much less corrosive than chlorine and iodine Sanitizers, so the chances of damage to surfaces are minimal. Quaternary Ammonia will properly sanitize stainless steel prep tables, the inside of commercial refrigerators, shelving, and other surfaces.

Quaternary Ammonium Sanitizer mixtures should be concentrated between 150 ppm and 400 ppm in 75-120 degree water. Like the other sanitizers, be sure to read the manufacturer's label and mix according to their directions and the health code regulations in your area. Quaternary Ammonium are easily dispensable from a wall mount above your three-compartment sink, whereas chlorine and iodine are not as easily dispensed. Always use test strips to determine if the sani water is at the right sanitation level. Change the water every 4 hours or as needed.

Set up all utensils, spatulas, grill scrapers, tongs and ladles. Make sure you have enough plates to get through the peak period. Stock all carryout containers, soufflé cups / lids and soup cups.

Check the stocking levels in the entire kitchen - refrigerator and freezer units. Check for expired date dots. Also make sure all products is rotated properly (FIFO). Make sure every employee working specific positions understand your expeditions and goals for the shift, talk them into position.

Every employee will be assigned a specific cleaning task & side work assessments. These assignments & cleaning task should be completed before the end of their shift. A manager needs to verify that the cleaning task and side work has been completed before the employee goes home for the day or night.

I recommend writing down the cleaning task and side work on an index card. When the employee arrives to work give them the card with the information on it, communicate your expeditions and time goals. Tell the employee the cleaning task and side work must be completed before the scheduled shift is done and that you must verify that the work has been completed.

Employees must meet the standard check times during the shifts and should apply sense of urgency.

Each employee will be assigned a specific work station position. These employees should be responsible for the upkeep throughout the shift and final breakdown. Stocking, date dots and detailed cleaning needs completed before the shift ends.

All utensils, spatulas, grill scrapers, tongs and ladles should be cleaned in the dishwasher and returned back to the kitchen for the next day's use. Having these tools ready for the opening shift saves time. The night time shift should set the daytime shift up for success.

All equipment needs thoroughly cleaned front, back, sides and inside. Floors under equipment needs swept and deck scrubbed. The back walls need cleaned nightly. The stainless steel wall should be degreased nightly, then polished.

Hood vents should be taken down and ran through the dishwasher nightly. Hood vents need to be taken down at the close, when there are customers in the restaurant the vents need to be in place. Let the vents, air dry overnight on a countertop, the opening shift will put the vents back in place before the hood fans are turned on.

All kitchen equipment should be turned off before you are done with the shift. All garbage cans should be emptied and relined. Once a week all trash cans need thoroughly cleaned and sanitized.

Cleaning the fryer

At the end of each shift the fryer should be filtered. When the oil begins to smoke or when you place a fryer basket in the fryer and you can't see the bottom of the fryer basket it is time to change the fryer oil. You can use fryer test strips to determine when to change the oil. Low volume restaurants can get away with changing the fryer oil once a week. Higher volume restaurants should change the fryer oil at a minimum twice a week. Use boil out once a week to thoroughly clean the inside of the fryer. When you empty out the oil from the fryer fill the fryer up with warm water. Turn the fryer on 350°F. Use the correct amount of boil out for each fryer. The fryers will boil. If the water begins to rise submerge a fryer basket into the fryer as this will bring the water level back down.

A manger should check you out before you are done with your shift.

Kitchen Training
Kitchen Position Training

BOH position training is the most important part of the training in many ways.

Before any other training is done the trainee has to be exposed to each position so if there are any calls outs and if the sales were higher than the projected forecast sales than the manager can bail out any position so that guest service is not jeopardized.

It will be necessary that the manager or employee train as a cook for at least 7 to 14 day's mainly because the manager or employee needs to know the menu and how to cook each menu properly. Seasoned cooks will take less time to learn how to cook your restaurant's menu and therefore will need less training.

Let's put it a different way, how are you going to serve food to the guest if by chance the cook calls out?

Are you okay with closing the restaurant for one day because you have no cook? That is why the manager or employee needs to know how to cook each item on your menu. Now depending how complex your menu is the trainee may need more or less training.

There are so many topics to learn:

Learning how to cook the food consistently: proper plate presentation and timing of foods

Learning and master each cooking position:
- Window selling station
- Grill station
- Fryer station
- Appetizer station
- Salad station
- Hot station
- Cold station (sandwiches and cold sides)
- Expeditor position
- Prep station
- Time & temperature, serving safe food and sanitation
- The importance of timing of the foods
- First in, first out (FIFO) and day dot procedures
- Opening & closing the kitchen (each shift sets up the next shift for success)
- Clean as you go
- Security & safety

During the training process for each position utilize the kitchen training sign-off sheet.

On the first day of training the trainee should shadow the trainer. This will allow the trainee to actually see how things are done. The trainer sets the tone for the training process. There cannot be any half stepping, training must be done correctly and consistently. To cook the food consistently is to know the menu inside and out. During the peak times it is recommended that the trainee shadow the trainer, this will ensure ticket times are not jeopardized.

During the off peak times is the most effective way to train, when training concentrate in one area at a time don't flip flop this will only confuse the trainee.

After the first day, let the trainee work that position. The trainer will shadow, observe, correct or commend the employee throughout each day. The trainee will not learn if he or she is shadowing you on the second day and beyond.

Throughout the training you should be asking questions and receiving answers. If the trainee gets the answer wrong, correct him or her, let a few minutes go by and asked that same question again until he/she gets it right, then commend him/her. This is a great memory tool and if done in this format the trainee will not forget that question. Make a game out of it and have fun.

Another great tool is to have a recipe binder in the area for quick reference.

In so many cases in restaurants all over the United States most trainees are thrown into a chaotic, dysfunctional kitchen.

This is not good for business; in fact, why even keep your restaurant open because you will lose money due to:

- Guests receiving poor service
- Customers spreading the word of mouth to friends & family of the poor experience
- Rotating door of employee's due to inadequate training
- Cooks receiving poor training which equals food mistakes
- Employee's quitting because they are not comfortable with a dysfunctional kitchen. Which creates on-going training and in return revenue loss because you have to train another cook. It makes perfect sense to stick to a good training program.

All cooks and servers need to be properly trained in every position; we are not a soup kitchen. We are a restaurant serving great tasting served fast.

Please refer to the recipe binder (cook's bible). In this binder each recipe has pictures and product build charts. Each plate needs plated up correctly with the rim of the plate wiped clean with a separate sanitized cloth. Food needs to be of quality and hot. Serve it the way you would expect to receive it.

The last line of defense is the person who serves the food to the guest, is the food hot? Is the food of quality? Is the rim of the plate clean? Scrutinize the plate and be very picky after all the guest is paying for it.

The cook that placed the finishing product in the food pick up window should advise either the expeditor or servers that the food needs delivered to the guest immediately. The golden rule of thumb is as soon as the food touches the food window, then the food must be delivered to the customer immediately.

Getting the servers and cooks organized is the key to your customers satisfaction. What causes long check times:

- Employees not trained properly
- Kitchen functionality
- Call-outs
- Management not trained in the kitchen or not helping the kitchen when they need help
- Poorly staffed
- No sense of urgency

Cross train all your cooks, this will be beneficial when other cooks need help. Train management in every restaurant position specifically cooking. When the kitchen falls behind in check times, then management needs to bail the kitchen out by jumping in and help get the checks back to standard check times.

Creating a menu recipe chart with illustrations of the menu products will prove to be beneficial in training your employees. The current cooks can also use the recipe book as a cheat sheet.

Make 3 copies of the recipe book:
1. **First copy**: Store this copy in the kitchen to be used as a recipe cheat sheet.
2. **Second copy**: Store this copy in the training room for your new hires.
3. **Third copy**: Store this copy in the manager's office as a backup recipe book.

To learn more about recipe guides and product build charts go to:

http://www.workplacewizards.com/restaurant-menu-recipe-guide/

If your cooks use the recipe book properly and consistently, the staff will consistently cook food correctly according to the recipe.

This helps the customer know that they are getting consistent quality food, no matter who is preparing the food for that particular shift.

Once you have recorded all your recipes into this recipe guide, place each recipe in a protective clear sheet. Place all recipes in a binder and utilize them as a training tool or as a quick reference chart.

Make sure you save the restaurant menu recipe guide as a master copy. Create the recipe guide from the master copy for each of your restaurant recipes

Train your employees to learn how to build menu products from top to bottom while in the process of preparing the food. The employees need to basically memorize the menu recipes and how to build each product correctly. This process will definitely help build consistency in your employees cooking habits.

The training employee must demonstrate timing of food

The Timing of the food is very important mainly because it is the difference between serving hot quality food or inferior cold food. How many times have you been at a fast food restaurant? How many times did you receive cold fries? Another issue is when the cooks prepare the entrees they are placing it under the heat lamp waiting for the vegetables to cook and in the meantime the entree is dropping in temperature.

Timing means everything

A properly trained cook will time their dishes perfectly. Let me explain further, the wheel person (lead cook) just called off two burgers to the grill person and the burgers will take approximately 2 ½ per side to cook. Almost immediately the lead person tells the fry person to drop one order of fries because it will take four minutes to cook the fries. By the time the fries are done the burgers will be done cooking, everything needs to go up together piping hot and fresh in the food pick up window.

Primarily, it will be the lead cook's responsibility to monitor the other cooks to ensure everything is perfectly timed.

Let me tell you what I have observed in some kitchens and what cooks do to create chaotic situations. They are not doing it purposely it's how they were trained.

The cooks have a total of 5 tickets hanging on the rail and three of those tickets have entrée's sitting in the window, all three are missing items that are associated with all three tickets. The cook is now just starting to work on the last two tickets, what is wrong with this picture? Bits and pieces of food are going up in the window, although nothing was sold. In the meantime, the quality of the food and the temperature of the entrées are going down the tubes.

The Remedy

Ticket number one just printed and the line cook placed it on the rail, he called out to the grill person saying, "**adding on**" two burgers and one chicken breast to be placed on the grill. Just then, another check printed it was for three more burgers and a sandwich melt (Patty melt) the lead cook communicates to the grill person and says "**add on**" four more burgers and a patty melt set up, at that time the lead person communicates to the grill by saying are there six burgers "**all day**" on the grill along with one patty melt?

The grill person confirms and communicates back to the lead cook saying "heard". The lead cook asked the fryer person if he or she has seven orders of french fries cooking "all day" and the fryer person tells the lead cook yes. It's all about communication and timing the food and organizing yourself and the other cooks.

Here is an eye opener

The typical order of french fries weight is 5oz. Let's say in an eight hour period, we wasted eight orders of french fries totaling 40oz. A 10 Lbs. case of french fries is 480 oz. There are six bags of fries to a case and each bag of french fries weighs 80 ounces each. If each portion bag of french fries weight was 5oz the total portions of fries per case are 96 portions.

Let's say, each portion sold for $2.50 a portion, which would mean we lost $20.00 in french fries for the day. That was based on the eight portions of french fries that were wasted.

In a week, we lost $140.00. One Month typically is 30 to 31days; we now lost $600 to $620. In 365 days (one year) is we now lost between $7200 to $7440 just in french fries and that is the selling prices to the guest. Of course the price we paid for it was lower.

Here is another eye opener

We lost eight portions of french fries in one day. In 365 days we have lost 2920 portioned fries, which equals 30 cases. At this rate, we will be out of business with just french fries alone. French fries are only one of many items on the menu. The lesson to be learned, don't waste any food.

When there are no tickets 5 things should happen:
- Restocking
- Sweeping
- Wipe down the area (Clean as you go)
- Cleaning assignments
- Prepping food

Never leave your station during any peak time. Breaks and smoke breaks never happen during peak times. If you do need to leave make sure the manager is aware of it.

Never argue with anyone, be the better person bite your tongue and wait until after the peak time and flag down a manager. Please make sure when you speak to a manager it is away from other employees and customers.

Food handling is a big responsibility. Having someone getting sick from eating at your restaurant is every restaurant owner's worst fear. No one wants to feel responsible for causing the suffering someone experiences from unsafe food.

A Restaurant's reputation is one of its most valuable assets, not to mention the possibility of a lawsuit for medical care and damages awarded to someone who gets food poisoning from your restaurant.

Everyone on your staff needs to know and understand how and why foods need to be kept at a certain temperature.

Keep cold food below 40°F hot food must be held at 145°F or above. If these temperatures are not kept, bacteria can multiply rapidly.

Keep a temperature log and check the temperatures of your freezer, cooler and hot and cold holding units. Include a thermometer calibration log as well to make sure your thermometer is functioning correctly.

It's a **"MUST DO"** Taking & recording food temperatures with an accurate stem thermometer is a critical element to insure your restaurant, your employees, and your chain are serving SAFE FOOD to our customers. It takes just a few minutes a day.

- If Managers, owners or franchises require temperature recording to be a daily routine, there are several benefits:
- Safer, wholesome better tasting food
- Shelf life of foods will be extended by knowing exactly how your food temperatures run from day to day
- Less food waste by maintaining correct food temperatures
- A great daily learning tool to build food safety skills for crew / employees
- Improved results on health inspections and internal company quality reports
- Faster awareness of refrigeration maintenance problems
- The very best defense in the case of a foodborne illness complaint your restaurant and/or chain will move into a HACCP-oriented method of complete food safety. H.A.C.C.P. (Hazard Analysis Critical Control Point) is a dynamic system being used in food processing and food service to help food managers and food workers identify and control potential problems before they happen. It is a very systematic approach based on controlling time, temperature, and specific factors that are known to contribute to food borne disease outbreaks. H.A.C.C.P requires record keeping as one of the important steps to make the system work.
- Hang or locate the charts in the appropriate work area on clip boards (not in a manager's office). Retain the completed records for at least 60 days in a 3 ring binder (the food safety experts suggest 6 months).

What can you do to serve safer food to your guest?

Employees need to know why it's important to wash their hands before handling food and the right way to wash their hands. Many instances of food contamination leading to illness can be traced to employees not washing their hands after using the restroom and then handling or serving food.

Use gloves properly, washing your hands before you put them on and before changing to new ones. You can never wash all of the bacteria from your hands and when you have gloves on, your hands sweat, causing the bacteria to multiply rapidly.

Personal hygiene is extremely important for food workers. Employees with cuts, abrasions, dirty hands and fingernails, skin diseases should not handle or serve food. Allowing sick employees is a temptation; especially if you are busy and short on staff, but the potential risk of infecting other people far out-weigh the inconvenience it can cause. Providing employees with free vaccinations can be a good investment, especially with regards to hepatitis.

Always wash all fruits and vegetables and never store bags or boxes of fruit or vegetables on the floor. Mop water contaminates food stored this way.

Make sure your water source is safe. Many restaurants have gone out of business because they used well water that was contaminated with bacteria.

Maintain the proper hot water temperatures when washing dishes and make sure your plates, silverware and glasses are clean and dry before stacking. Wet dishes can be breeding grounds for bacteria.

Hire an exterminator to keep pests under control. Rodents and insects can spread disease and contaminate food. Since garbage cans are breeding grounds for pests, keep lids on them and wash them often.

Policy

The temperatures of all potentially hazardous hot foods will be taken during preparation and service to ensure safety of food served to children. All hot foods will be prepared using appropriate practices and procedures to ensure safety and sanitation.

Procedures

Employees involved in the production of food must complete the following steps:

Prepare hot foods: Cook hot foods to these minimum endpoint temperatures or higher

Food Product	Internal Temperature
Poultry	165ºF for 15 seconds
Stuffing, stuffed meats,	165ºF for 15 seconds
Casseroles and other dishes	165ºF for 15 seconds
Combining raw and cooked foods	165°F for 15 seconds
Ground or flaked meats	155°F for 15 seconds
Beef roasts; pork roasts and chops	145°F for 3 minutes
Beef steaks, veal, lamb	145°F for 15 seconds
Commercially raised game animals	145°F for 15 seconds
Fish and foods containing fish	145°F for 15 seconds
Shell Eggs (for immediate service)	145°F for 15 seconds
Vegetables (canned, frozen, fresh)	140°F for 15 seconds
Potentially Hazardous Foods	140°F for 15 seconds
Cooked in microwave for 2 minutes	165°F, then let food stand
After cooking	165°F, then let food stand

Guidelines for hot food:

- Take endpoint cooking temperatures.
- Record the endpoint cooking temperature on the time, temperature log.
- Use batch cooking to reduce holding time of foods.
- Allow the temperature of cooking equipment to return to required temperatures between batches.
- Do not use hot holding equipment to cook or reheat foods.
- Heat fruits, vegetables, and ready-to-eat (RTE) commercially processed and packaged foods to 140°F for hot service.
- Prepare foods at room temperature in two (2) hours or less, or the food item should be returned to the refrigerator. **A TOTAL** time of food at room temperature shall not exceed 4 hours. This includes time spent in receiving, assembly, and holding.
- Prepare raw products away from other products not receiving heat treatment. This reduces the opportunity of cross contamination with any ready-to-eat food.
- Maintain food contact surfaces:

Kitchen Training
Cross Contamination

What is Cross Contamination?

The process by which bacteria or other microorganisms are unintentionally transferred from one substance or object to another, with harmful effect. Just because you can't see Bacteria or Viruses does not mean they don't exist – they are so small the human eye can't see it. See separate manual pertaining to Bacteria & Viruses and Fungi for further information. For more information on cross contamination go to: http://www.foodsafety.gov/

The said fact is, everything is dirty from counter tops to the human hands; it's what we do to minimize the chances of spreading germs from our hands to the guest food.

Let's start with the kitchen, Sanitation buckets with Quat Sanitizer is recommended at most restaurants, towels need to be kept in the sanitation buckets when not being used. The sanitation buckets need to be changed often, especially if the water is dirty. Sanitation test strips should be used. PPM (150-400 Parts per Million) All surfaces, especially around foods needs to be sanitized every 4 hours or when the surface is dirty.

Gloves need to be worn by all food service workers at all times. Gloves need to be changed when:

- Touching raw meat, chicken or fish
- Touching face or hair
- Touching any part of your uniform, including your apron
- If there is a rip in the gloves
- Using the restroom
- Every four hours

This particular topic is so important because there are so many foodborne illnesses that can spread purely because either we did not wear gloves and or did not wash our hands frequently.

How to Prevent Cross Contamination

Cross-contamination can create many unsafe issues on a restaurant kitchen. In fact, depending on the extent of contamination, it can shut your entire operation down. But don't fear. There are things you can do to prevent those little microscopic bacteria from stealing your thunder, and subsequently, your profits.

Simply make sure that you and your staff follow these cross-contamination prevention tips.
- Store foods separately
- Store and refrigerate raw foods separately from ready-to-eat foods.
- Keep raw meats in well-sealed containers on the bottom shelf of your refrigerator.
- Store raw foods on shelves below ready-to-eat foods to minimize contamination from accidental drips or other contact.
- Prepare foods separately
- Prepare foods on clean, separate surfaces to minimize the spread of germs.
- Utilize clean cutting boards as safe surfaces for preparing foods.

If possible, designate individual cutting boards for different types of foods. This can be done easily with color-coded cutting boards.

How to Prevent Cross Contamination

Implement Proper Hand Washing Procedures:

- All staff members should properly wash hands, which mean washing both hands and forearms with hand soap for two minutes. Use a scrub brush to clean under the nails and don't forget to wash between the fingers. Dry hands with a disposable paper towel.
- Take the time to wash hands between tasks.
- Give special attention to washing hands before and after handling raw foods as these are particularly potent carriers of bacteria.

Make Personal Hygiene a Priority:

- Keep clothes, hair, and other personal items away from all food preparation areas. Wear head coverings and gloves. Keep facial hair clean and well-groomed.
- Take extra care when coping with personal illness. If a staff member is even remotely sick, send them home immediately. Sneezing and coughing can easily spread germs to food and get other staff members sick.

Clean as You Go:

- Clean between tasks
- Use hot, soapy water to clean all supplies, equipment, utensils, and surfaces between food preparation tasks.
- Avoid using the same dish or utensil to handle raw and cooked foods. Use one utensil and dish for raw foods and one utensil and dish for cooked foods.
- Sanitize Properly
- Sanitizer provides an extra defense against the transfer of germs and allergens.

There are 3 types of Sanitizers that can be used in restaurants or bars

Chlorine Sanitizers

Chlorine Sanitizers are used in both the FOH and BOH. Chlorine Sanitizers should have a minimum concentration of 50 ppm (parts per million) and a maximum of 200ppm in 75-100 degree water. Read the manufacturer's label and check the local health code to see which concentration is required for your restaurant or bar.

Iodine Sanitizer

Many bars use iodine-based Sanitizers to clean glasses. This is because it leaves less flavor and smell than a chlorine sanitizer, however, it's not good to use on porous surfaces. Cutting boards, wooden utensils, and any other porous surfaces will absorb the color and permanently stain. Iodine-based Sanitizers are less common and somewhat more expensive than chlorine-based Sanitizers. They aren't as effective, but they are less irritating to the skin and less likely to cause an allergic reaction. You can tell how strong an iodine sanitizer is by how deep its color is when mixed with water. The darker the brown, the stronger the mixture.

Iodine-based Sanitizers should be concentrated between 12.5ppm and 25ppm in 75-120 degree water. Note that the hotter the water, the more unstable the chemical becomes. However, the cooler the water, the longer the chemical mixture must be allowed to sit on the surface being cleaned. Kitchen surfaces should never be wiped with cloth towels, unless the towels are dry and used only for that specific purpose.

Quaternary Ammonia

Quaternary ammonium Sanitizers (Quat) are great for sanitizing kitchen walls, floors and countertops. They are much less corrosive than chlorine and iodine Sanitizers, so the chances of damage to surfaces are minimal. Quaternary Ammonia will properly sanitize stainless steel prep tables, the inside of commercial refrigerators, shelving, and other surfaces.

Quaternary Ammonia Sanitizers must be left to air dry on the surface of what is being cleaned. In a commercial kitchen setting, buckets of Quaternary Ammonia Sanitizer should be placed in easily accessible areas with dry, clean rags nearby. Rags should not be stored in the sanitizer as food particles from used rags can render the sanitizer useless.

Quaternary Ammonia Sanitizers protect against organisms that promote food spoilage, which is why they work well in refrigerated areas. A Quaternary Ammonium Sanitizer is good for disinfecting handrails, pagers, door knobs and other surfaces that customers touch to prevent contraction of the flu virus.

Quaternary Ammonium Sanitizer mixtures should be concentrated between 150 ppm and 400 ppm in 75-120 degree water. Like the other sanitizers, be sure to read the manufacturer's label and mix according to their directions and the health code regulations in your area. Quaternary Ammonium are easily dispensable from a wall mount above your three-compartment sink, whereas chlorine and iodine are not as easily dispensed.

Kitchen Training
Color Coded Cutting Boards

Use color-coded cutting boards for all products:

- Red for meat
- Green for vegetables or fruits
- Yellow for raw chicken
- Brown for seafood.
- White for Dairy.
- Blue for cooked foods

Clean and sanitize all food contact surfaces, cutting boards, and utensils that have been used in the preparation of raw meats, poultry, and fish prior to using for raw fruits and vegetables and ready-to-eat foods. Cleaning and sanitizing steps MUST be done separately in order to be effective.

Take temperatures:

- Use a calibrated thermometer to take the temperatures of all food products.
- Wipe the thermometer stem with alcohol wipes prior to and after taking the temperatures of each food; or wash stem, rinse, and sanitize.
- Take temperatures in the thickest part of a food item (usually the center). Two readings should also be taken in different locations to assure thorough cooking to the appropriate endpoint temperature.
- Record the endpoint cooking temperature on the **time, temperature log.**

Serving the food to the guest is the last process in the flow of food, before the guest receives the food it needs to be 100% safe;

Did you follow the steps correctly (flow of food) from beginning to the end?

It is very important that we follow these steps as a team to prevent the guest getting sick or dying. Ultimately, if this occurs, you are putting your business in jeopardy. As a manager it is our responsibility to monitor and train the crew in these areas.

Kitchen Training
Cleaning vs. Sanitizing

Knowing the difference between cleaning and sanitizing is a must in order to prepare your restaurant for health inspections. The basic idea is this: cleaning removes what you can see, and sanitizing removes what you can't. Cleaning dishes and equipment means washing off food particles, dirt, oils, and other visible materials.

Sanitizing requires the use of specialized agents that attack and kill bacteria and germs. While detergents are readily available in any Grocery store or drug store, you'll need to purchase

Sanitizers that is specific to your needs, such as dishwasher sanitizer and glassware sanitizing tablets, at restaurant supply stores.

A liquid Quat sanitizer designed to sanitize previously cleaned surfaces and equipment.

To Sanitize food processing equipment, utensil and other food contacts:

- Scrape, flush, or presoak articles and thoroughly wash articles with an appropriate detergent or cleaner. Rinse thoroughly with potable water.
- Sanitize articles by immersing articles with a use-solution of 2 ounces of this product per 2 7/8 - 7 3/4 gallon of water (0.25 - 0.68 ounce of this product per gallon of water) (150 - 400 ppm) (or equivalent dilution) for at least 60 seconds.
- Remove immersed items from solution to drain and then air dry. Non immersed items should be allowed to air dry. Do not rinse

Keep your restaurant's dishes clean and sanitary:

- When using chemical Sanitizers, be sure the water is not over 120 Degrees Fahrenheit, or the chemicals will evaporate.
- Three-sink setups are required for effective cleanup. One sink is for washing one for rinsing, one for soaking in sanitizing mixture.
- Let dishes air dry or let them dry in the dishwasher's cycle. If you must hand-dry, do not use anything but clean rags to dry dishes.

Both low and high temperature dish machines need hot, soft water to wash dishes. Although NSF requires low-temperature dish machines only need be provided with a minimum water temperature of 120 degrees F, we recommend 140-150 degrees F incoming water temperature and then to 180 degrees F to comply with NSF sanitizing rinse requirements. As normal rated flow pressure of 20 pounds per square inch (psi), the common single-tank.

When it comes to food rotation everyone needs to get involved The Cooks and Servers & Managers.

Let's start with the flow of food pertaining to FIFO. As the delivery truck gets put away everything needs rotated from new to the back and old to the front.

First used stickers are recommended: They are big lettered stickers it's kind of hard to miss it. Food should be put away on the shelves left side (New Product) right side (Old Product) or rotated from new to the back and old to the front.

Labels need to be facing towards you. It might be a good idea to carry a black marker so you can mark the cases that are hard to read or missing labels. No foods should ever be stored on the floor; they need to be 6 inches from off the floor.

Storage shelves need to be NSF approved (Certified Food Equipment).

What is NSF?
NSF International was formerly known as the National Sanitation Foundation. It is a not for profit organization that provides public health and safety risk management solutions. Among those solutions, NSF International provides standards development and product certification. Foodservice and restaurant supply products that are certified by NSF undergo and have passed an evaluation to ensure that the product and facility where the product is made meet NSF standards for food safety. NSF standards are generally accepted by government regulatory agencies.

Kitchen Training
Date Dots

I have been in restaurants that use date dots and restaurants that don't. I strongly suggest using date dots, why?

- It helps to identify what needs to get used first.
- It helps reduce food waste and spoilage.
- It helps to reduce the guest from getting sick or dying.

By not using date dots will put your restaurant at risk of shutting down or worse sued due to a fatality. If a guest gets sick and they report it to the health department they are required to come out and inspect your restaurant and that you do not want they don't just look for the source they will scrutinize your entire establishment and to make it worse it is possible you will read about it in the newspaper, that is a Restaurant killer.

Part of the prep cooks and line cooks responsibility is to be using date dots on all food products.

The manager should always checkout the prep cooks before they leave for the day or night.

What do the managers look for when checking out the prep cooks and line cooks?

- Prep sheet filled out correctly and consistently.
- The prep cooks and line cooks prepped the correct amount of foods according to the prep sheets.
- The use of date dates on all food products with the correct information on them.
- Proper use of rotation of all foods (FIFO).
- All foods are properly covered.
- All storage rooms which includes: refrigerated and freezer units, dry storage and the prep area is clean, organized and sanitized.
- All storage containers, pots and pans are stored on a food approved shelf and is inverted.
- All preparation utensils, tongs, spatulas and ladles are stored in a food approved area and are inverted.

Kitchen Training
Date Dots

The manager on duty should always consistently throughout the shift and day verify that the prep cooks and cooks are properly labeling food with date dots. See the below illustration of the proper procedure on how to use date dots.

The metal/ plastic insert pans located on the hot & cold holding units should also have date dots. The salad station containers and dressing containers should also have date dots on them.

See the below chart for a complete list of product shelf life's from A to Z

A Standard Date Dot

Example of a properly completed date dot

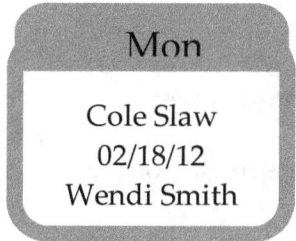

Always use the actual shelf life of any product when completing date dots

Kitchen Training
Refrigerator Layout

All refrigerated and frozen storage areas of a restaurant require a thermometer inside. This even applies to small refrigerated reach-ins on the cook's line and server's line and refrigerated grill drawers.

For restaurant walk-in refrigerators:

- Top Shelf - Prepared foods
- Below prepared foods - Fruits and vegetables
- Below Fruits and vegetables - Fish & seafood
- Below Fish & seafood - Beef & Pork
- Below Beef & Pork - Ground Meat
- Below Ground Meat - Poultry
- Lemons should be stored on the bottom shelf, separate from other foods
- Eggs to be stored on the bottom shelf
- Raw Beef to be stored on its own bottom shelf
- Raw chicken to be stored on its own bottom shelf
- Nothing should be placed on the floor of a refrigerator or freezer.
- Everything should be on a shelf at least six inches off the floor
- All foods and food storage containers should have a date dot on then to identify the shelf life of the product, the person's name and the date the item was prepared.

If you are storing food in an upright refrigerator, use large sheet trays to avoid spillage. Never store raw meats on top of other foods such as produce.

First in, first out (FIFO) always rotate foods in all storage areas.

Store raw meats on a lower shelf in a food approved storage container. **Use date dots**.

Food Shelf Life Chart

Product	Room Temperature (70° F)	Refrigerator (37° to 40° F)	Freezer (0 °F)	Comments
Breads, fresh	Store at room temperature. Use the date as a guide or use within 3 to 5 days.	Storing in the refrigerator promotes staling.	3 months	Over wrap well to prevent drying out; thaw at room temperature
Bread and rolls, unbaked dough		2 to 3 days	2 months	Sometimes dough doesn't rise as well if frozen
Bread Crumbs and Croutons	6 months			
Muffins, rolls, quick breads		3 days	1 to 2 Months	Wrap individually, pick in rigid containers to prevent crushing
Pancakes and waffles		2 days	1 month	Freeze with waxed paper between each two. Heat without thawing in a toaster or under broiler
Pastries, Danish, Doughnuts		Store at room temperature. Best used within 1 to 3 days	3 months	
Tortillas, corn or Flour		1 week	3 months	Wrap well
Tube cans of rolls, biscuits, pizza dough, etc.		Use-by-date	Don't freeze	
Ready-to-bake pie crust		Use-by-date	2 months	

Food Shelf Life Chart

Product	Room Temperature (70° F)	Refrigerator (37° to 40° F)	Freezer (0 °F)	Comments
Cakes				
Angel food & sponge cakes		3 days	4 to 6 Months	Wrap well
Cheesecake		3 to 7 days	4 to 6 Months	Wrap well
Fruit cakes			1 year	Wrap well
Layer cakes		Room temperature. Best used within 3 to 7 days	2 to 4 Months	Wrap well. Butter frosting freezes well, fluffy egg white frostings don't
Cookies				
Cookies, homemade and baked	2 to 3 weeks		4 to 6 Months	Pack in airtight container
Cookies, store bought and packaged	2 months		8 to 12 Months	
Cookies, unbaked dough		2 to 3 days	6 months	Form refrigerator dough cookies in rolls; wrap tightly, thaw in refrigerator before slicing or dropping on cookie sheets

Food Shelf Life Chart

Product	Room Temperature (70° F)	Refrigerator (37° to 40° F)	Freezer (0 °F)	Comments
Pies				
Chiffon pie, Pumpkin pie		2 to 3 days	1 month	
Cream and Custard Pies		2 to 3 days	6 months	
Fruit pies, baked		2 to 3 days	6 to 8 Months	Wrap well; thaw at room temperature; heat in 350°F Bake about 15 minutes
Fruit pies, unbaked			8 months	Cut holes in upper crust to vent; bake unthawed
Pies, starch-thickened Custard		1 to 2 days	Do not Freeze	Fillings become watery and lumpy and pastry becomes soggy
Pies, nut, baked		4 to 5 days	6 months	Wrap well
Pie shells, unbaked		1 day	2 months	Fit in pie pans; prick crusts. Stack pie pans with 2 layers freezer paper between. Place in freezer bags. Either bake frozen or thaw in refrigerator
Quiche		2 to 3 days	6 months	

Food Shelf Life Chart

Product	Room Temperature (70° F)	Refrigerator (37° to 40° F)	Freezer (0 °F)	Comments
Dairy Products				
Butter Margarine, Spread substitutes		1 to 3 months, unopened 2 to 3 weeks, opened 4 to 5 months, unopened 1 month, opened	9 months 1 year	Leave in original wrapping; overwrap well
Cheese, Hard (such as Cheddar, Swiss) Cheese, parmesan, grated Cheese Soft (such as Brie, camembert)		6 months, unopened 3 to 4 weeks, opened 1 week	6 months 1 to 2 months 6 months	It is recommended that you don't freeze cheese! Freezing destroys the Character of the cheese. If you do freeze, the cheese is best used in cooking; will crumble when sliced; thaw in refrigerator to minimize crumbling. Repackage in freezer bags
Cottage Cheese, Ricotta Cheese		1 week, opened 45 to 60 day, unopened	Doesn't freeze Well	Separates, becomes Grainy

Food Shelf Life Chart

Product	Room Temperature (70° F)	Refrigerator (37° to 40° F)	Freezer (0 °F)	Comments
Dairy Products				
Cream Cheese	Never expose cream cheese to room temp for more than 2 hours or 1 hr. at 90° F or higher.	2 weeks	Doesn't freeze Well	Can be mixed with other ingredients and frozen; by itself becomes crumbly.
Cream-Whipped, ultra-pasteurized Cream-Whipped, Sweetened Cream-Aerosol can, real whipped cream		1 month 1 day 3 to 4 weeks 3 months	Doesn't freeze 1 to 2 months Doesn't freeze Doesn't	Freeze small mounds of lightly sweetened whipped cream on cookie sheet. Then repackage so the mound won't be crushed. Thaw in refrigerator or serve frozen.

Food Shelf Life Chart

Product	Room Temperature (70° F)	Refrigerator (37° to 40° F)	Freezer (0 °F)	Comments
Fruit				
Commercially Frozen Fruits			1 year	
Canned Fruits		12 to 24 months, Unopened opened 2 to 3 days		Do not store in opened can. Store in airtight container.
Dried fruits	6 months	3 to 5 days, cooked		Keep cool, in airtight container; if possible, refrigerate
Apples		3 to 5 months		
Apricots, grapes, nectarines, peaches, pears, plums		3 to 5 days	6 months	See preserving instructions for individual fruits
Avocados	2 to 3 days after Ripened	5 to 10 days		
Bananas	Store at room Temperature			Freeze whole in skin or peel and mash; great in breads and cakes
Berries, cherries		2 to 3 days	Freeze individually on cookie sheets; repackage in heavy plastic bags	
Cranberries		3 to 4 weeks		8 to 12 months
Grapefruit	7 days	2 weeks	4 to 6 months	Wrap cut surfaces to prevent loss of Vitamin C.
Grapes		1 to 2 weeks		
Guavas, papayas		1 to 2 days		
Kiwi Fruit	3 to 5 days after Ripening	4 to 6 months if unripe.		

Food Shelf Life Chart

Product	Room Temperature (70° F)	Refrigerator (37° to 40° F)	Freezer (0 °F)	Comments
Fruits				
Lemons	1 week	2 to 5 weeks		
Limes	1 week	2 to 5 weeks		
Melons		1 week	8 to 12 months	Wrap cut surfaces to prevent Vitamin C loss and to control odors.
Oranges	3 to 4 days	5 to 6 weeks		
Peaches	Ripen at room Temperature	2 to 3 days		
Pineapple	1 to 2 days	3 to 5 days		
Tangerines	2 to 3 days	1 week		
Watermelon	Uncut watermelon can be stored at room temperature for a few days	6 to 8 days		
Fruit Beverages				
Juices in cartons, fruit drinks, punch		3 weeks unopened 7 to 10 days opened	8 to 12 months	

Food Shelf Life Chart

Product	Room Temperature (70° F)	Refrigerator (37° to 40° F)	Freezer (0 °F)	Comments
Meats				
Deli & Vacuum-Packed Products				
Store-prepared (or homemade) egg, chicken, ham, tuna, macaroni salads		3 to 5 days	Doesn't freeze well	
Hot dogs & Luncheon Meats				
Hot dogs, opened package unopened package		1 week 2 weeks	1 to 2 months 1 to 2 months	Changes texture, flavor Changes texture, flavor
Luncheon meats opened package unopened package		3 to 5 days 2 weeks	1 to 2 months 1 to 2 months	These lose flavor quickly; wrap tightly These lose flavor quickly; wrap tightly
Bacon & Sausage				
Bacon and pancetta		7 days	1 month	Leave unopened in original wrapping; over wrap well
Sausage, fresh; raw from chicken, turkey, pork, beef		1 to 2 days	1 to 2 months	Over wrap packages well
Smoked breakfast links, patties		7 days	1 to 2 months	Over wrap packages well
Hard sausage— pepperoni, jerky sticks		2 to 3 weeks	1 to 2 months	Keep in original packaging; over wrap Well
Summer sausage— Labeled "Keep Refrigerated"		opened 3 weeks unopened 3 months	1 to 2 months 1 to 2 months	

Food Shelf Life Chart

Product	Room Temperature (70° F)	Refrigerator (37° to 40° F)	Freezer (0 °F)	Comments
Ham, Corned Beef				
Ham, fully cooked vacuum sealed at plant, dated, unopened		"use by" date on package	1 to 2 months	
Ham, fully cooked, whole		7 days	1 to 2 months	
Ham, fully cooked, half		3 to 5 days	1 to 2 months	
Ham, fully cooked, slices		3 to 4 days	1 to 2 months	
Hamburger, Ground				
Hamburger, ground beef		1 to 2 days	3 to 4 months	Remove from supermarket wrapping; wrap well in freezer plastic wrap; over wrap with heavy-duty aluminum foil
Ground turkey, veal, pork, lamb & mixtures of them		1 to 2 days	3 to 4 months	Remove from supermarket wrapping; wrap well in freezer plastic wrap; over wrap with heavy-duty aluminum foil
Fresh Beef, Veal, Lamb, Pork				
Steaks		3 to 5 days	6 to 12 months	Wrap pieces individually, then over wrap tightly

Food Shelf Life Chart

Product	Room Temperature (70° F)	Refrigerator (37° to 40° F)	Freezer (0 °F)	Comments
Fresh Beef, Veal, Lamb, Pork				
Chops		3 to 5 days	4 to 6 months	Wrap pieces individually, then over wrap tightly
Roasts		3 to 5 days	4 to 12 months	Wrap pieces individually, then over wrap tightly
Variety meats-- tongue, liver, heart, kidneys, chitterlings		1 to 2 days	3 to 4 months	
Pre-stuffed, uncooked pork chops, lamb chops, or chicken breast stuffed with dressing		1 day	Don't freeze Well	

Food Shelf Life Chart

Product	Room Temperature (70° F)	Refrigerator (37° to 40° F)	Freezer (0 °F)	Comments
Soup & Stews				
Chili			4 to 6 months	All-meat chili freeze better than those containing beans, which can break down & become mushy
Soups, broth-based		3 to 4 days	4 months	Freeze in usable amounts or individual Servings
Soups, cream-based, such as chowders, bisques		2 days	Do not freeze	Can curdle and separate
Stock		3 to 4 days	4 to 6 months	Freeze in usable amounts
Stews		3 to 4 days	4 to 6 months	Freeze in usable amounts
Meat Leftovers				
Cooked meat and meat casseroles		3 to 4 days	2 to 3 months	
Gravy and meat broth		1 to 2 days	2 to 3 months	
Fresh Poultry				
Chicken, turkey, or duck, whole		1 to 2 days	1 year	Keep in original packaging
Chicken or turkey, Pieces		1 to 2 days	9 months	Over wrap well
Giblets		1 to 2 days	3 to 4 months	

Food Shelf Life Chart

Product	Room Temperature (70° F)	Refrigerator (37° to 40° F)	Freezer (0 °F)	Comments
Fresh Poultry				
Chicken, turkey, or duck, whole		1 to 2 days	1 year	Keep in original packaging
Chicken or turkey, Pieces		1 to 2 days	9 months	Over wrap well
Giblets		1 to 2 days	3 to 4 months	
Cooked Poultry				
Fried chicken		3 to 4 days	4 months	
Cooked poultry Casseroles		3 to 4 days	4 to 6 months	
Pieces, plain		3 to 4 days	4 months	Best frozen in stock, used in soups, casseroles
Pieces covered with broth, gravy		1 to 2 days	6 months	
Chicken nuggets, patties		1 to 2 days	1 to 3 months	

Food Shelf Life Chart

Product	Room Temperature (70° F)	Refrigerator (37° to 40° F)	Freezer (0 °F)	Comments
Pizza				
Pizza		3 to 4 days	1 to 2 months	
Stuffing				
Stuffing, cooked		3 to 4 days	1 month	
Fish				
Lean fish (cod, flounder, haddock, sole, etc.)		1 to 2 days	6 months	Remove from light supermarket wrap. Wrap well or use ice method below.
Fatty fish (salmon, bluefish, mackerel, salmon, etc.)		1 to 2 days	2 to 3 months	Place on cookie sheet, loosely covered with foil. Freeze. Dip in water several times; freeze to form thin ice glaze; wrap well; over wrap well
Cooked fish		3 to 4 days	4 to 6 months	Texture becomes mushy
Smoked fish		14 days or date on vacuum package	2 months in vacuum package	Vacuum package
Shellfish				
Clams, oysters, scallops; live			7 to 10 days	Remove from shells. Freeze in their own liquid in airtight plastic freezer bags or containers; raw scallops easily become rubbery
Cooked shellfish		3 to 4 days	3 months	
Crab, cooked		1 to 2 days	2 months	If in shell, leave in shell; dip in water and freeze to form thin ice glaze to prevent drying out and becoming stringy; then repackage

Food Shelf Life Chart

Product	Room Temperature (70° F)	Refrigerator (37° to 40° F)	Freezer (0 °F)	Comments
Shellfish				
Clams, oysters, scallops; live			7 to 10 days	Remove from shells. Freeze in their own liquid in airtight plastic freezer bags or containers; raw scallops easily become rubbery
Cooked shellfish		3 to 4 days	3 months	
Crab, cooked		1 to 2 days	2 months	If in shell, leave in shell; dip in water and freeze to form thin ice glaze to prevent drying out and becoming stringy; then repackage
Fish Sticks			18 months	
Lobster tails, raw			3 months	
Lobster & Crab, live		same day purchased		

Food Shelf Life Chart

Product	Room Temperature (70° F)	Refrigerator (37° to 40° F)	Freezer (0 °F)	Comments
Shellfish Continued				
Shrimp, crayfish, squid, shucked clams, & mussels; raw		1 to 2 days	3 to 6 months	Dip in water, freeze, to form ice glaze; place in freezer plastic bags
Shrimp, cooked			Don't freeze	Texture becomes mushy
Shrimp, breaded, commercial				1 year
Staples or Pantry Items				
Baby Food, canned	12 months, unopened 2 days, opened			
Baking Powder	18 months, unopened 6 months, opened			Keep dry and covered.
Baking Soda	2 years, unopened 6 months, opened			Keep dry and covered.
Barbecue Sauce	1 year, unopened	6 months, Opened		
Biscuit Mix	12 to 18 months			
Bouillon Cubes or Granules	2 years			Keep dry and covered.
Brownie Mix	9 to 12 months			
Cake Mix	9 to 12 months			
Candies		2 to 4 Months	6 months	Chocolate-coated varieties may develop white bloom on outside from temperature; thaw in refrigerator
Catsup/Ketchup, Chili Sauce, Cocktail Sauce	12 months, unopened 1 month, opened			Refrigerate for longer storage

Food Shelf Life Chart

Product	Room Temperature (70° F)	Refrigerator (37° to 40° F)	Freezer (0 °F)	Comments
Staples or Pantry Items				
Chocolate Syrup	2 years, unopened	opened - 6 months		Cover tightly and refrigerate after opening
Cocoa Mixes Cocoa, Baking	8 months, unopened 3 to 6 months, opened 24 months			Cover tightly
Coconut, shredded (canned or packaged)	unopened - 1 year	opened - 6 months		Refrigerate after opening
Coffee, cans Coffee, instant Coffee, whole bans	unopened - 2 years unopened - 1 to 2 years opened - 2 months 1 to 2 weeks			Storing coffee at room temperature is the most convenient method of storage. It works well for coffee that will be consumed within one to two weeks of purchase.
Cornmeal	18 months			Keep tightly closed
Cornstarch	Indefinite			Keep tightly closed
Crackers	6 months		3 months	Freeze "sleeves" in heavy plastic bags
Flour, white Flour, whole wheat Flour, bread	6 to 8 months 6 months 6 to 8 months	1 year 1 year	1 to 2 years 1 to 2 years 1 year	Store in refrigerator
Gelatin, all types	18 months			Keep in original containers
Grits	12 months			Store in airtight container

Food Shelf Life Chart

Product	Room Temperature (70° F)	Refrigerator (37° to 40° F)	Freezer (0 °F)	Comments
Staples or Pantry Items				
Herbs, dried Herbs, fresh	6 to 12 months	1 week	1 to 2 years	
Honey	12 months, unopened and opened			Cover tightly. If crystallizes, warm jar in pan of hot water
Horseradish	1 year, unopened	4 to 6 months		
Hot Sauce	3 years			
Jelly, Jam & Preserves	unopened - 12 months	opened - 6 months		Refrigerate after opening
Maple Syrup	1 year, unopened	3 years, opened		
Marshmallow Cream	unopened - 3 to 4 months			
Marshmallows	2 to 3 months			Keep in airtight container
Mayonnaise	unopened - 2 to 3 months	opened - 2 to 3 months		Refrigerate after opening
Molasses	unopened – 12 months opened – 6 months			Keep tightly closed. Refrigerate to extend storage life.
Mustard, prepared Yellow	unopened - 2 years opened 6 to 8 months			May be refrigerated. Stir before using.
Nuts (Nuts; hazelnuts, walnut, pecans), in Shell Nuts, vacuum can	4 months 3 months	1 year	2 years	Refrigerate after shelling. Freeze for longer storage.
Milk (condensed or evaporated, canned	12 months +			Invert cans every 2 months

Food Shelf Life Chart

Product	Room Temperature (70° F)	Refrigerator (37° to 40° F)	Freezer (0 °F)	Comments
Staples or Pantry Items				
Milk, non-fat dry	unopened - 6 months opened - 3 months			Store in airtight container
Olives, bottled or canned	1 year			
Pancake Mixes	6 to 9 months			
Pasta (dry spaghetti, macaroni, etc.)	2 years			Once opened, store in airtight container
Peanut Butter	unopened - 6 to 9 months opened - 2 to 3 months			Refrigeration not necessary, but will keep longer if refrigerated.
Pectin, liquid Pectin, dry	opened - 1 month unopened - 1 year 1 year			
Pickles	unopened - 1 to 2 years			
Pie Crust Mix	unopened - 8 months			
Popcorn	1 to 2 years			Keep in airtight container
Potatoes, Instant	6 to 12 months			
Pudding Mixes	12 months			
Rice, white Rice, flavored or herb	2 years + 6 months			Keep tightly closed
Salad Dressings, bottled	unopened - 10-12 months opened -3 months			Refrigerate after opening
Salad Oils (corn, canola) Olive Oil	18 months 24 months			

Food Shelf Life Chart

Product	Room Temperature (70° F)	Refrigerator (37° to 40° F)	Freezer (0 °F)	Comments
Staples or Pantry Items				
Sauces & Gravy Mixes	6 to 12 months			
Shortening	unopened - 18 months opened - 6 to 8 months			
Spices, whole Spices, ground	1 to 2 years 6 to 12 months		2 to 3 years 1 to 2 years	Store in airtight container in a dry place.
Sugar, granulated Sugar, brown Sugar, confectioners or Powdered Sugar, sweeteners	2 years + 4 months 18 months 2 years +			Put in airtight container and cover tightly
Syrups	12 months			Keep tightly closed. Refrigerate to extend storage life.
Tea, bags Tea, instant Tea, loose	18 months 3 years 2 years			Store in airtight container
Tofu		1 week	5 months	Change storage water every day or two after opening.
Vanilla Extract	2 years, unopened 2 months, opened			Keep tightly closed
Vinegar	2 years, unopened 12 months, opened			Keep tightly closed and store in a cool, dark area.
Yeast, dry or frozen compressed Vacuum-sealed bag	Package expiration date Indefinitely		1 to 2 years	

Food Shelf Life Chart

Product	Room Temperature (70° F)	Refrigerator (37° to 40° F)	Freezer (0 °F)	Comments
Vegetables				
Commercially Frozen			8 to 12 months	Store in original package
Canned Vegetables	1 year	3 to 5 days, opened		Do not store in the opened can. Store in airtight container.
Artichokes		1 week		
Asparagus		3 to 5 days	8 to 12 months	
Beets, carrots		2 weeks	8 to 12 months	
Beans, broccoli, lima beans, peas, summer squash		3 to 6 days	8 to 12 months	
Bell Peppers		1 to 2 weeks	3 to 4 months	Freeze raw, slice in strips or dice
Cabbage		1 week	Do not freeze	To watery to freeze well
Cauliflower		1 week	8 to 12 months	
Celery, chilies		1 week	8 to 12 months	
Corn		Use immediately for best flavor	8 to 12 months	
Garlic bulbs Garlic cloves, individual	3 to 4 months 5 to 10 days		You can freeze whole, unpeeled heads and remove cloves as you need them	Store in a cool, dark, and dry location (dampness is the enemy of garlic, so store away from stove and sink).
Green onions		3 to 5 days	Do not freeze	Become limp
Greens: collards, kale, mustard, spinach, Swiss chard		3 to 5 days	8 to 12 months	

Food Shelf Life Chart

Product	Room Temperature (70° F)	Refrigerator (37° to 40° F)	Freezer (0 °F)	Comments
Vegetables				
Green beans		1 week	8 to 12 months	
Lettuce and salad greens		1 week	Do not freeze	Too watery; becomes limp
Mushrooms		1 to 2 days	8 to 12 months	Slice thinly and sauté first, otherwise they become rubbery and lose flavor
Radishes		2 weeks		
Squash, hard	3 to 6 months			

The Manager or the lead cook needs to be responsible for checking the truck off, mainly because there are so many issues that can occur such as

- Outdated product.
- Spoiled product.
- Distribution center shorted you a case.
- Time & temperature abuse.

As you are checking the truck, look for the above issues. All frozen and refrigerated products need to be stored in the freezer or walk in immediately.

If you find ice crystals forming on any frozen foods do not accept it demand a credit.

Ice Crystals
Ice crystals Indicate an item was refrozen. If an item was not placed directly in the freezer at the distribution level, it is possible the item started to thaw. Once the item was placed back into a freezer, ice crystals develop. Never ever accept that delivery, it may pose serious health risk to your guest.

On the next page you will find information on meats, poultry, and fish and with what to accept and not to accept.

Canned goods
Never accept bloated cans or dented cans. Never accept cans with no labels or labels on the wrong product. Never accept rusted cans. And most of all never accept outdated cans.

Produce
Never accept foods that are not constituted as fresh. Signs of non-quality product; bruised or discolored, slimy, wilted or the product has a strong odor.

Never accept foods that are bruised or discolored. Make sure you physically go through each case of produce and only accept quality product.

Dry goods
Look for holes in boxes (indicates that rodents were present) also look for rodent droppings. Look for expiration dates.

Inspect your food after all it's your money can you really afford **cash in your trash.**

Inspecting your Meat, Poultry & Fish

Employees need to know when to accept or not accept certain foods when delivered to the restaurant.

Food service operators are becoming proactive in their approach to cold food management. Most restaurants have scheduled temperature checks, both ambient and core, for all foods in refrigerated environments. Managers and chains are also requiring a log of regular temperature checks from their distribution network.

Though the trend is spreading, not all distributors are taking accurate temperature readings. If this is the case, simply rely on your other senses and reference the following table to know what to accept and what to reject:

Protein	Temperature	Accept	Reject
Fresh Beef Fresh Lamb Fresh Pork	40°F or lower 40°F or lower 40°F or lower	Color: bright, cherry Color: bright red Color: white fat, pink	Brown, green or purple splotches Black, white or greenish spots Cartons are broken Meat wrappers are dirty or torn
Fresh Poultry	40°F or lower	Texture: firm and springs back when touched	Purple or green discoloration around neck Darkened wing tips Abnormal odor Stickiness under wings and joints Soft, flabby flesh
Fresh Fish	40°F or lower	Eyes: bright, clear and full Texture: flesh and belly are firm and spring back When touched Packed with self-draining ice	Fishy or ammonia odor Eyes sunken, cloudy or red-bordered Dry gills Flesh is soft and gives Finger imprint stays if pressed into Flesh
Fresh Shellfish	45°F or lower for live 0°F or lower for frozen		Shells are partly open and do not close when tapped Soft shell Strong odor

Kitchen Training
Flow of Food

The Flow of Food is a term commonly used in the restaurant industry to describe how food moves from purchasing to serving through a food service establishment. At each of the nine stages, food must be handled properly.

Follow the flow of food:

1. Receiving food from the truck
2. Storing the foods in the freezer, walk-in and dry storage
3. Thawing food properly
4. Prepping foods
5. Cooking foods
6. Hot & cold holding
7. Reheating foods
8. Cooling foods
9. Serving the foods to the guest

1. Purchasing and Receiving

All food must come from approved sources. Homemade or uninspected food is not allowed. Inspect all incoming food for torn, damaged or stained Boxes. Inspect the condition of the delivery truck. Check the temperature of incoming food. Refrigerated foods must be at 4ºC (40ºF) or less. Frozen food must be at -18ºC (0ºF) or less

2. Storage

Practice F.I.F.O. (First In, First Out). Store chemical products away from food products. When foods are repackaged, clearly label and date container. All food containers must be properly covered.

Refrigerated Storage

All refrigeration units must have an accurate indicating thermometer. Temperatures must be maintained at 4ºC (40ºF) or less. Store all raw foods below cooked or ready to eat foods to prevent cross contamination. Avoid packing refrigerator full, air needs to circulate to maintain proper temperature. Use NSF approved storage shelving.

Freezer Storage

Must be maintained at -18ºC (0ºF) or less. Use NSF approved storage shelving. Make sure all foods are properly covered.

Dry Storage

Keep food at least 15cm (6in) off the floor to facilitate cleaning and to easily identify rodent problem. Temperature must be at 72°F. Discard cans that are dented or have bulges. Also discard cans that have no labels on them. Use NSF approved storage shelving.

3. Thawing food
There are three acceptable ways to thaw foods.

- Thaw foods naturally from the freezer to the walk in.
- Under flowing water (not to exceed 70F)
- Microwave - defrost cycle; Raw food defrosted should not be refrozen;
- Use item within 2 days.

Never leave food in room temperature to thaw. When prepping foods always prep one item at a time. When you are done prepping that particular item store the item into the walk-in, then continue on to the next item and so on. Always clean as you go and organize before, during and after the food prepping process.

Also, any foods that sit at room temperature will start to grow bacteria and they will multiply as the foods get warmer and it is suggested that any foods sitting in room temperature (4 Hours) or more be thrown away, food should never sit at room temperature.

4. Prepping Foods
Wash your hands before beginning preparation and in between tasks. Prepare food in small batches. Prevent cross contamination by cleaning and sanitizing utensils and work surfaces in between tasks, or by using color coded cutting boards for different foods. Prepare the food as close to serving time as possible.
Set up the following prior prepping foods:

- Plastic spatulas, ladles, scoops, tongs, mixing bowls and knives
- Measuring devices: measuring cups, measuring spoons, portion bags, portion containers, cutting boards and scales.
- Food approved storage containers and date dots.

Prep cooks are responsible for the rotation of all products every time they are in a room they need to rotate foods. A good rule to practice for a prep person is only prep what the day calls for. Have all the necessary utensils, bowls, measuring cups ready to go.

Prep only one item at a time and when you are done clean and sanitize the area, then move on to the next prep item. Also, as they are prepping food items, proper day dots need to be used consistently as they are putting away the food, that's were first in first out (FIFO) comes in.

Just before the prep cook leaves for the day the manager should verify that all the prep was done correctly. The managers should also check the refrigerator, freezer and dry storage to ensure that the food on the shelves are rotated (FIFO) properly. You should also verify that all items contain a properly filled out date dot on them. All counter tops and shelves cleaned and sanitized. Floors swept and trash cans emptied/relined. All containers, utensils and cookware are stored (vertically) on the shelves.

5. Cooking

Cooking Temperatures (Internal Temperatures)

Whole Poultry (Chicken & Turkey)	82°C	180°F
Poultry Pieces or Ground Poultry	74°C	165°F
Hazardous Food Mixtures	74°C	165°F
Ground Meats (Beef, Pork, Lamb)	71°C	160°F
Fish	70°C	158°F

Use a Probe Thermometer to check for cooking temperatures. Temperature to be maintained for a minimum of 15-Seconds.

Microwave Cooking

- Hot and cold spots – if there is no rotating base in the microwave physically stop the cooking process and turn the food occasionally. The internal temperature needs to be at 165°F or 15 seconds before removing it from the microwave.
- Check internal temperature at 3 different sites.
- Place thicker portions of food toward the exterior of the microwave dish.
- Ensure the containers are microwave safe.

6. Hot Holding

Food should be cooled from 60ºC (140ºF) to 4ºC (40ºF) within 4 to 6 hours. It can take hours, if not days, for large quantities of food to cool to appropriate temperatures.

Suggestions of how to reduce cooling times:

- Place pots of food in an ice water bath.
- Divide large quantities of food into smaller containers 10cm (4in) in depth.
- Stir frequently.
- Slice or divide large cuts of meat into smaller pieces
  Place in the refrigerator and once it cools to 4ºC (40ºF) cover the container.

Proper Hot Holding

- Maintain temperature of hazardous food above 60°C (140°F).
- Check internal temperature of the food using a metal stem probe thermometer every 2 hours.
- Never cook or reheat food in hot holding equipment

7. Cold Holding

Keep food cold in refrigerated display units or on ice. The internal temperature of the food must be maintained at 4ºC (40ºF) or less.

Cooling Foods

The general rule: Foods that need time and temperature control for safety (TCS food, for short) must be cooled from 135°F (57°C) to 41°F (5°C) or lower within six hours.

First, cool food from 135°F to 70°F (57°C to 21°C) within two hours. Then cool it from 70°F to 41°F (21°C to 5°C) or lower in the next four hours.

If the food hasn't reached 70°F (21°C) within two hours, it must be reheated and then cooled again. If you can cool the food from 135°F (57°C) to 70°F (21°C) in less than two hours, you can use the remaining time to cool it to 41°F (5°C) or lower. However, the total cooling time cannot be longer than six hours.

8. Reheating

- Reheat cold hazardous food to original cooking temperature.
- Reheat quickly on or in the stove.
- Never reheat slowly over several hours in hot holding units.
- Place food on the stove or in the microwave to reheat, and then place in hot holding units.

9. Serving

- Prevent cross-contamination by ensuring servers take appropriate personal hygiene measures (e.g. Handwashing, no direct contact with food).
- Ensure clean and sanitized utensils are used.
- Do not stack plates when serving meals to customers.
- Ensure service areas kept clean, and regularly wipe down menus.

If transporting foods, ensure vehicles are clean and foods are held at proper hot or cold holding temperatures.

I cannot stress enough that food safety is everyone's responsibility. If someone gets sick or dies from eating at your restaurant you are liable and one of the risks is a lawsuit. In fact, you may not survive after being sued. That is a restaurant killer. Be proactive and protect your employees and customers from food borne illnesses. Practice food safety.

The allergic food reaction may be caused by:

- Peanut, Tree Nuts, Milk, Eggs, Wheat, Soy, Fish, Shellfish

Mild symptoms may include one or more of the following:

- Hives (reddish, swollen, itchy areas on the skin)
- Eczema (a persistent dry, itchy rash)
- Redness of the skin or around the eyes
- Itchy mouth or ear canal
- Nausea or vomiting
- Diarrhea
- Stomach pain
- Nasal congestion or a runny nose
- Sneezing
- Slight, dry cough
- Odd taste in mouth
- Uterine contractions

Severe symptoms may include one or more of the following:

- Obstructive swelling of the lips, tongue, and/or throat
- Trouble swallowing
- Shortness of breath or wheezing
- Turning blue
- Drop in blood pressure (feeling faint, confused, weak, passing out)
- Loss of consciousness
- Chest pain
- A weak or "thread" pulse
- Sense of "impending doom"

Severe symptoms, alone or in combination with milder symptoms, may be signs of anaphylaxis and require immediate treatment.

Clean as you go

Keep the kitchen and your workstation clean and organized at all times. Sometimes during the rush times it gets very busy and the only focus is selling food. We understand that, when the rush times slow down clean up the kitchen and workstation along with a floor sweep. Try to keep your area as clean as possible between each guest check that you sell. Before leaving for the day or night the kitchen should be fully stocked food rotated and check for expired date dots. All equipment should be clean and sanitized and the floor swept. Garbage emptied and relined. All side work and cleaning task completed. A manager must check you out prior to you leaving the shift.

Severe symptoms, alone or in combination with milder symptoms, may be signs of anaphylaxis and require immediate treatment.

What is Anaphylaxis?

Anaphylaxis (anəfəˈlaksis) is a severe, potentially life-threatening allergic reaction. It can occur within seconds or minutes of exposure to something you're allergic to, such as a peanut or the venom from a bee sting.

The flood of chemicals released by your immune system during anaphylaxis can cause you to go into shock; your blood pressure drops suddenly and your airways narrow, blocking normal breathing.

Signs and symptoms of anaphylaxis include a rapid, weak pulse, a skin rash, and nausea and vomiting. Common triggers of anaphylaxis include certain foods, some medications, insect venom and latex.

Anaphylaxis requires an immediate trip to the emergency department and an injection of epinephrine (ep-uh-nef-rin,-reen) If anaphylaxis isn't treated right away, it can lead to unconsciousness or even death.

Clean as you go

Keep the kitchen and your workstation clean and organized at all times. Sometimes during the rush times it gets very busy and the only focus is selling food. We understand that, when the rush times slow down clean up the kitchen and workstation along with a floor sweep.

Kitchen Training
Grill Cooking Procedures

The trainee must demonstrate all grill cooking procedures and the timing of all foods. The employee also should know how to scrape the grill frequently to prevent carbon build up on food products especially sandwiches.

Breakfast grill temperature – Eggs (275°F),
Pancakes and french toast (350°F).
Lunch and dinner grill temperatures (350°F).

The employee should recite by memory the correct build too on all food products and ingredients including any sauces or side items that come on the side. Grill grease drawer & hood grease pan needs emptied frequently to prevent spillage. The employee should know where to find grill products in the kitchen and in the walk-ins. The employee also should know about date dot procedures and rotation, first in, first out **(FIFO).**

Any product that needs to be trashed needs to get management approval and recorded on to the waste for tracking purposes.

Employees need to restock the area prior to any peak time period and throughout the shift, especially at the end of the shift. Grill area needs to clean and organized at all times. Basically the employee needs to master the position.

Grill: Hamburger Cooking Procedures

When cooking a hamburger, make sure you handle the meat safely. Wash your hands before and after handling the ground beef.

After about 3 to 4 minutes of cooking time, check the burger for doneness. Place an instant-read in the center of the thickest burger. According to the USDA, ground meat must be cooked to at least 160°, or well done. This typically takes from 4 to 5 minutes, depending on the thickness or size of the hamburgers.

After using the food thermometer, clean it with hot soapy water.

Though any temperature under 160° is not considered safe for ground meat (USDA Guidelines), here is a list of cooking times for varying degrees of doneness for burgers:

- Rare: 120 to 125
- Medium Rare: 130 to 135
- Medium Well: 150 to 155
- Well Done: 160 to 165

Always scrape the grills before and after each use to prevent carbon and grease build up.

Equipment:
1. Several pairs of 6 inch or longer metal tongs
2. Pastry brush
3. Small metal butter pan
4. Large metal mixing bowl
5. Two grill dome lids
6. Grill char broil chicken season
7. Small plastic squeeze water bottle
8. Plastic squeeze bottle filled with melt pan: oil pan/grill. This is a buttery liquid that you can brush on the grill and chicken during the cooking process.

Always use thawed chicken (never frozen)

How to properly thaw chicken:

Place frozen chicken into a designated NSF approved container with a strainer and lid. It will take approximately take 2 days to thaw in the refrigerator walk-in. Use date dots on each storage container. Must have the person's name on the date dot along with the date it was prepped and the name of the product in the container.

How to determine how much product to thaw:

The use of the pull thaw sheet will allow you to determine the right amount of product to pull from the freezer to the refrigerator without running out of food for your guest. This sheet is a PAR sheet. More info: http://www.workplacewizards.com/restaurant-pull-thaw-sheet/

Season the flat top grill prior to cooking. Make sure the grill is clean and there is no carbon build up on it. Make sure you pound the meat prior to placing them on a hot grill. Drip a small amount of melt pan oil onto the grill, then place the chicken directly on top of the melt pan. Cover the chicken with the grill dome lid. Cook approximately 2 minutes, then flip the chicken over and cook for an additional 2 minutes. During the second cooking process, squeeze some water from the water bottle directly under the dome where the chicken is cooking.

Remember to cook the chicken for 2 minutes per side, total cooking time 4 minutes. The internal temperature of the chicken must be at 165°F.

Add flavor before you grill

The best part of grilling is the ritual of throwing it onto the grill and relaxing with a drink while it cooks. Take a little extra time to inject flavor into the chicken before grilling so you can skip basting and don't have to do much work as it grills, and you know the end flavor will be amazing. Try a brine, rub, or marinade, it doesn't have to be fancy at all!

Stay away from high heat

Chicken is not steak or burgers, where you want a fairly high heat to get a good sear on the outside. Since chicken needs to cook thoroughly and you don't want the skin to burn, it's wise to cook it over medium heat, indirect heat for most of the cooking time. For a charcoal grill, this may mean building a two-level fire or only having coals on half of the grill, and for a gas grill, a medium heat works best.

Servers, when a guest orders a steak, especially a medium well or well done steak, please advise the guest that it will take longer to prepare the steak than normal.

Managers and grill cooks should always have a thermometer on hand, below is the cooking doneness chart.

Use a thermometer to accurately temp the product for doneness

Steak Doneness	Remove from grill at this temperature	Final cooked temperature
Rare	130 to 135 degrees F	130 to 140 degrees F
Medium rare	140 degrees F	145 degrees F
Medium	155 degrees F	160 degrees F
Well done	165 degrees F	170 degrees F

Buy the Best
The most tender and flavorful steaks are Prime grade, but you won't see them often at the grocery store. The next best quality is Choice. Good selections in the Choice grade are filets, rib eyes and porterhouse steaks. If you have access to a butcher, take advantage of their expertise. There are ranges within each grade and a butcher will know if your steak is at the top end of the Choice grade or the bottom. The top of the range will give you beef that's very close to Prime quality.

Warm It Up
Make sure the steak is at indoor room temperature. If you put a cold steak on the grill, the exterior will burn before the interior cooks to the desired temperature. Do not let the steak sit at indoor room temperature for more than an hour before cooking.

Oil the Meat, Not the Grill
Spray oil is a griller's best friend when it comes to cooking steak or any kind of skinless protein. An evenly applied coating of neutral oil such as vegetable or canola on both sides of the steak will ensure the steak doesn't stick to the grill.

Get It Hot
Preheat your grill on high. And then do the hand test. Hold your hand over the grates. You shouldn't be able to leave it there for more than two seconds. You want to hear that sizzle when the steak hits the grill. That high heat will give your steak a perfect crust.

Know When It's Done

This is the most nerve-wracking aspect of learning to grill the perfect steak. Invest in a digital meat thermometer. It will take all the guesswork out of knowing when your steak is done. For a rare steak, the internal temperature as measured in the middle of the steak is 125 degrees. For medium rare, it's 130-135 degrees and well done is 155 degrees.

Let It Rest

Never cut into a steak that's hot off the grill. Pull it off the heat, tent it with foil and let it rest about 8 minutes. While it is resting, the steak's fibers will relax, the juices will redistribute back to the center and the temperature will come up.

Tip: If your steak is around 2 inches thick, it will continue to rise in temperature even when it's off the grill. A good rule of thumb is to pull it off five degrees before target.

The muscle fibers in fish are constructed of very short bundles (up to ten times shorter than the long muscle fibers in meat). And, compared to meat, fish muscle contains only a small fraction of connective tissue, which sits in very thin sheets perpendicular to the muscle bundles. What does this all mean? To put it plainly, fish are more sensitive to heat!

Here are some Thermos Works recommended temperatures for a few of our favorite cuts:

Salmon – 125°F
Salmon like all fish has almost no collagen, which means it will start to lose moisture quicker than beef. While the FDA recommends cooking fish to 145°F, for a flakier, more moist and tender salmon filet many chefs find that it's best enjoyed when it's cooked to medium 125°F.

Halibut – 130°F
Halibut is a very firm fish and holds together well in cooking. This makes it particularly good for grilling. Too often it is overcooked and dry, the center should be just becoming opaque. It is done when it reaches an internal temperature between 130 and 135°F.

Lobster – 140°F
Cooking lobster is straightforward. But like most all seafood, due to its tightly-bound muscle structure and lack of the lubricating fat that makes cooking meat a more forgiving process, lobster cookery can go wrong easily. You want to cook lobster just through. Cooking it too much makes for a rubbery, dry and unfortunate situation, and too little will result in an odd texture and undeveloped flavors. When grilling, many sources* recommend cooking lobster to a minimum internal temperature of 140°F and serving immediately. However, when boiling or steaming, Cook's Illustrated suggests taking the internal temperature to 175°F, because the muscle fibers in lobster are longer and require more heat to shrink.

Scallops – 130°F
Because scallops are a lean protein source they should be cooked quickly under high heat and require some fat (such as oil or butter) during cooking. Cook to 130°F internal temperature until the flesh is milky white or opaque and firm.

Shrimp – 120°F
Constriction is the telltale sign that you've overcooked your shrimp. The longer you cook them, the tighter and tougher they will get. Look for a change in color (light pink) and an internal temperature of 120°F to tell you when your shrimp are ready to come off the heat. A miniature needle probe is perfect for checking the internal temperature of shrimp.

Ahi Tuna – Rare – Below 115°F
Tuna is most often served rare or seared rare because the longer you cook it, the more flavor and moisture it loses. Tuna cooked rare is optimal in order to maintain flavor and moisture. Raw tuna frequently carries a parasite, but "Sashimi" grade fish has been flash frozen to kill any parasites. Restaurants that serve raw tuna are required to use Sashimi grade.

Commercial Grills are some of the most versatile pieces of cooking equipment in the restaurant they can be used to cook anything from eggs to steak on a single cooking surface without worrying about flavor transfer. However, if that cooking surface is not properly seasoned and maintained, the food coming off of the grill plate will not be very tasty.

Seasoning a Commercial Grill

Food is placed directly on the commercial grill surface to cook, and the only way to assure that food does not stick to the grill plate is to properly season it. In this respect, seasoning does not refer to flavor.

Instead, it is a process by which oil or lard is baked onto the metal to create a non-stick surface on which to cook. New grills and those that have been extensively cleaned will require seasoning. Also, if the food starts sticking, it is time to re-season the grill. Follow these steps to season your commercial grill:

- Wipe the grill surface clean with a lint-free cloth.
- New grills: Light all of the burners and turn them on a low setting (around 300 °F) for an hour. Let it cool before proceeding to the next step.
- Rub cooking oil, shortening, beef suet or baking soda on the grill with a lint-free cloth. Heat the grill to 350 – 400 °F.
- When the grill reaches the desired temperature (red light turns off), turn off the grill and allow it to cool.
- Wipe off excessive oil and repeat steps 3 – 5 one more time.

The need for re-seasoning depends on how often the grill is used, but you can expect to re-season the grill at least once a week, usually after a weekly deep-cleaning. If the food starts sticking, you will need to re-season the grill more often.

If you are only using one grill, set one side at (275ºF) for eggs and set the other side at (350ºF) for French toast and pancakes.

2 grills – Set the first grill at: (275ºF) for eggs. Set the Second grill at (350ºF) for French toast and pancakes. Remember to scrape the grill before and after each use.

83

It is important to cook eggs thoroughly to destroy bacteria. While light cooking will begin to destroy any bacteria that might be present only proper cooking brings eggs to a high enough temperature to destroy them all. For eggs, the white will coagulate (set) between 144 and 149° F, the yolk between 149 and 158° F, and whole egg between 144 and 158° F.

Egg products made of plain whole eggs are pasteurized, or heated to destroy bacteria. The pasteurization process consists of bringing the eggs to 140°F and keeping them at that temperature for three and a half minutes. While this temperature destroys bacteria, it does not thoroughly cook the product.

For scrambled eggs, omelets and frittatas, cook eggs until no visible liquid remains. Fried eggs should be cooked until the whites are completely set and the yolk is thickened but not hard.

For classic poached eggs, cook gently in simmering water until the white are completely set and the yolk begins to thicken but are not hard. Avoid precooking and reheating poached eggs.

Hard cooked eggs should reach an internal temperature of more than 160°F. After cooking, cool hard-cooked eggs under water or in ice water. Immediately after cooling, refrigerate eggs in their shell and use up to one week.

Other foods that contain eggs, like French toast, quiches, make sure that the dishes are done and prevent uneven cooking by using a thermometer in the center and around the sides of the of the dish. The thermometer should reach 160°F

84

Kitchen Training
Fryer Station

The employee must demonstrate all fryer cooking procedures. Fryer temperature should be set at (350°F) for breakfast, lunch and dinner.

Most fryers will have a timer built into the unit – All that is needed is for you to program each timer to each specific fried food.

The fryer temperature should be set at 350ºF. Most appetizer foods such as Mozzarella Cheese Sticks or Fried Zucchini will be fried to a golden brown texture.

French Fries
(350ºF) 4 to 4-1/2 minutes, fried to a golden brown texture.
Drain and salt immediately after cooking. Never batch cook fries, cook per order to avoid waste.

Chicken Strips:
Fry at: (350°F) for 5 to 6 minutes to a golden brown texture. The product will float when done.

Battered Shrimp:
Drop shrimp into hot oil and fry for 30-60 seconds or until golden brown.
The product will float when done.

Fried Shrimp:
Fry at: (350ºF) for 2 to 3 minutes or until golden brown in texture. Cook until it is golden brown in texture. Typically the product will float when it is done in most cases.

The employee should recite by memory the correct build too on all food products and ingredients including any sauces or side items that come on the side.

The employee should know where to find grill products in the kitchen and in the walk-ins. The employee also should know about date dot procedures and rotation, first in, first out (FIFO).

Any product that needs to be trashed needs to get management approval and recorded on to the waste for tracking purposes.

Employees need to restock the area prior to any peak time period and throughout the shift, especially at the end of the shift.

Fryer area needs to be cleaned and organized at all times. Basically the employee needs to master the position.

Kitchen Training
Hot Station Position

The employee must demonstrate all hot station cooking procedures. The hot station temperature should be set at (350°F). Use a 5" Probe Thermometer to proper temp the hot station water. Frequently check to see if the water level in the hot station is where it needs to be. Heating elements will burn up if there is not enough water in the unit. Turn on the unit one hour prior to use to ensure the water temperature reaches (350°F).

Heat all products prior to storing them onto the hot station (165°F) for 15 seconds. Frequently temp the product (every two hours) to ensure it is at the proper temperature (135°F) or above. If the product falls below (135°) you must reheat the product back to (165°F) for 15 seconds either by using the microwave, stove top, convection ovens, or double boilers.

The employee should recite by memory the correct build too on all food products and ingredients including any sauces or side items that come on the side. The employee should know where to find the hot station products in the kitchen and in the walk-ins.

The employee also should know about date dot procedures and rotation, first in, first out (FIFO). Any product that needs to be trashed needs to get management approval and recorded on to the waste for tracking purposes. Employees need to restock the area prior to any peak time period and throughout the shift, especially at the end of the shift. The hot station area needs to be cleaned and organized at all times. Basically the employee needs to master the position.

Recommended thermometers and its uses

- **5" Probe Thermometer** - Temp meats, hot foods in steam tables and hot liquids from - 0°F to 220°F.
- **Deep Fry Thermometer** - This thermometer, specially designed deep fried items, has a 2" wide dial that has a temperature range from 100 to 400+ degrees Fahrenheit.
- **Infrared Thermometer** - Accurately measure the temperatures of your cold foods with the infrared thermometer. This item is a safe, non-contact infrared thermometer perfect for measuring surface temperatures. This thermometer has a temperature range between -67 and 428 degrees Fahrenheit or -55 to 220 degrees Celsius so you can get an accurate reading on everything from ice cream to boiling soups and more.

Recommended website for your restaurant supply needs: **http://www.webstaurantstore.com/**

Kitchen Training
Cold Station (Sandwiches & Cold Sides)

The employee must demonstrate all **cold station & (sandwich)** procedures. The trainee should demonstrate on how to correctly construct a quality sandwich quickly (sense of urgency).

The training manager/employee needs to understand on how to read customer checks. Servers may abbreviate the foods that are listed on the check, all employees should know how to read the abbreviations. Using abbreviations while the server takes the orders will cut down the amount of time it takes to write down the order and also will cut down on paper cost. The cooks will be able to read the checks quickly and accurately if the checks are abbreviated.

Priority checks are very important. Appetizer checks have priority over all guest checks and need to be prepared within 7 minutes or less and served to the guest before all other foods. As the appetizer checks print on the kitchen printer, these checks need to be placed ahead of all other checks. Makes these checks lead checks to be prepared.

At times, the food is sent back to the kitchen for various reasons: wrong item was made, hair in food or non- quality product. Whatever the reason is this check is now a priority check and it needs to be made and delivered to the guest as quick as possible (sense of urgency). When foods are sent back, never microwave or reheat the foods, always give the guest a freshly made item. If the cook failed to send out hot quality food to the guest and it was sent back for whatever reason, the guest will expect what they paid for "fresh quality food served fast and correctly".

The employee should recite by memory the correct build too on all food products and ingredients including any sauces or side items that come on the side. The employee should know where to find the cold station products in the kitchen and in the walk-ins.

The employee need to be trained not to tear open any breads as this will cause the item to go stall which equals cash in the trash. The employee also should know about date dot procedures and rotation, first in, first out **(FIFO).** Any product that needs to be trashed needs to get management approval and recorded on to the waste for tracking purposes.

Employees need to restock the area prior to any peak time period and throughout the shift, especially at the end of the shift. The cold station area needs to be cleaned and organized at all times. Basically the employee needs to master the position. A great idea is to have backups of your key items and stored them below inside the cold station. Make sure these backups have a date dot on them and are rotated. Cover each backup container to prevent objects falling into them.

Kitchen Training
Salad Position

The employee must demonstrate how to prepare a salad quickly and correctly.

Side salads should be prepared and delivered to the guest within 4 minutes. Salad entrées should be delivered to the customer when all other entrées are delivered to that specific table. Entrées normally will take about 15 minutes or less to prepare unless the guest orders steaks or foods that take longer to prepare. The server should advise the customer if they order an item take require longer preparation time, it may take longer to prepare and deliver the entrées.

The manager and employee's should recognize fresh quality product. Inspect each salad, side or salad entrée to ensure quality: no wilted or brown colored lettuce, no slimly tomatoes or cucumbers. It is very important that the guest receives what they paid for "fresh quality product". If you fail, then repeat business fails.

The employee should recite by memory the correct build too on all food products and ingredients including any sauces or side items that come on the side.

The employee should demonstrate proper plating procedures.

The employee needs to demonstrate teamwork. Help out in other kitchen positions, including helping out in the dish room when needed. The employee should know where to find the salad station products in the kitchen and in the walk-ins.

The employee should be able to visually detect any quality issues with produce, any signs of deterioration or browning of product should not be used.

Any product that needs to be trashed needs to get management approval and recorded on to the waste for tracking purposes. The employee also should know about date dot procedures and rotation, first in, first out **(FIFO)**.

Employees need to restock the area prior to any peak time period and throughout the shift, especially at the end of the shift. The cold station area needs to be cleaned and organized at all times. Basically the employee needs to master the position before excelling to another training position.

Kitchen Training
Appetizer Position

The employee must demonstrate all appetizer procedures. All fried foods must have **a** golden fried texture. The cook must demonstrate the proper plating procedures, garnishes and sauces.

The employee should recite by memory how to correctly build all food products and ingredients including any sauces or side items that come on the side.

Appetizers should take 7 minutes or less to prepare and delivered to the guest. Appetizer checks are priority checks and need to be lead checks on the kitchen check rail. The employee should know where to find the appetizer station products in the kitchen and in the walk-ins.

The fryer temperature needs to be set at 350°F. If the fryer has smoky fumes or when you place the fryer basket inside the fryer and you can't see the bottom of the basket, it is time to change the oil. You can prolong changing the oil by filtering the oil at the end of each shift.

This will defiantly save you money and you will be delivering quality product to your customers.

Any product that needs to be trashed needs to get management approval and recorded on to the waste for tracking purposes.

The employee also should know about date dot procedures and rotation, first in, first out **(FIFO).**

Employees need to restock the area prior to any peak time period and throughout the shift, especially at the end of the shift.

The employee needs to demonstrate teamwork. Help out in other kitchen positions, including helping out in the dish room when needed.

The appetizer station area needs to be cleaned and organized at all times. Basically the employee needs to **master the position** before excelling to another training position.

Kitchen Training
Window Lead Person Position

The window person is actually selling the food to the guest by plating the food and placing them into the window. Prior to selling the food double check the kitchen ticket up against what is actually on the plate to ensure that there is nothing missing.

Hot food hot, cold food cold. If there is no steam coming off the food please reheat the item back up to (165°F) for 15 seconds. This is to prevent customer complaints and getting back up in the kitchen because you have to remake the food.

Plate presentation is another factor that creates eye appealing food that the guest wants and deserves. Every plate that leaves the kitchen with food on it should have **a** clean plate rim.

The window person plays a huge role in running a smooth kitchen. If supplies are needed the window person delegates the task to other employees. The window person never leaves his or her area. This is to ensure that the main focus on selling food is not compromised. The window person also communicates to the other employees clean as you go and frequent floor sweeps. Basically, they are in charge of the entire kitchen staff during any given shift.

The employee must demonstrate all plating procedures and build too. The window person as the tickets print on the kitchen printer they must communicate back to the fryer and grills and other positions what items need to be dropped to start the cooking process or prepared.

The grill and fryer stations and other stations will echo back to the window person that they understood the communication **"heard"**. Please remember about how to properly time the foods, this is to ensure all foods come up together hot and fresh. Remember Employee should recite by memory the **correct build too** on all food products and ingredients including any sauces or side items that come on the side.

The employee should know where to find the all kitchen product items in the kitchen and in the walk-ins.

Any product that needs to be trashed needs to get management approval and recorded on to the waste for tracking purposes. The employee also should know about the date dot procedures and rotation, first in, first out **(FIFO).** Employees need to restock the area prior to any peak time period and throughout the shift, especially at the end of the shift. The cold station area needs to be cleaned and organized at all times. Basically the employee needs to master the position before excelling to another training position.

Plate Presentation
Clockwise: protein (meat) starch, then vegetable.

All plated foods that leaves your kitchen needs to be checked for proper plate presentation and garnishes. Put your feet into your guest shoes and see what they see "a quality appealing plate". A sanitation bucket with a clean towel should be available to ensure the rim of each plate is clean.

Expeditor Position

This is a very important position, in-fact this is the last line of defense before the guest receives the food. The expeditor normally works the opposite end of the window person facing the kitchen area. The expeditor may have a ticket rail to hang guest checks. The expeditor main objective is to sell the food by either running it to the guest table themselves or by assigning a food runner to complete that task.

The expeditor ensures that whatever is on the guest checks matches with what is on each customer's plate. Proper plate presentation and garnishes play a huge role in an eye appealing presentation to the guest. Make sure you have fresh garnishes prior to any meal period.

There should be back-up of fresh garnishes in the walk-in if needed. Date dots need to be placed on each container to ensure proper rotation and quality of product. If the container of garnishes is sitting at room temperature, then the container should be sitting in an ice bath (Time & Temperature). If there is no food runner every employee should be responsible in running food to the customers, this will prevent inferior food quality or falling food temperatures.

Time and Temperature

The temperature danger zone is: temperatures between 41 °F and 135 °F.

Time Temperature Control for Safety (TCS)

Is a way to control effective safety measures. Improper time and temperatures may create unsafe food consumption and may cause food Bourne Illness.

Leaving food out too long at room temperature can cause bacteria (such as Staphylococcus aureus, Salmonella, Enteritis's, Escherichia Coli and Campylobacter to grow at dangerous levels that can cause illness. Bacteria grow most rapidly in the range of temperatures between 40 °F and 140 °F, doubling in number in as little as 20 minutes.

Keep Food Out of the **"Danger Zone"**

Never leave food out of refrigeration over 2 hours. If the temperature is above 90 °F, food should not be left out more than 1 hour.

- Keep hot food hot **at or above 140 °F**. Place cooked food in chafing dishes, preheated steam tables, warming trays, and/or slow cookers.
- Keep cold food cold **at or below 40 °F**. Place food in containers on ice.

Cooking Foods

Raw meat and poultry should always be cooked to a safe minimum internal temperature. When roasting meat and poultry, use an oven temperature no lower than 325 °F. If you aren't going to serve hot food right away, it's important to keep it at 140 °F or above.

Storing Leftovers

One of the most common causes of foodborne illness is improper cooling of cooked foods. Bacteria can be reintroduced to food after it is safely cooked. For this reason leftovers must be put in shallow containers for quick cooling and refrigerated at 40 °F or below within two hours.

Reheating

Foods should be reheated thoroughly to an internal temperature of 165 °F or until hot and steaming. In the microwave oven, cover food and rotate so it heats evenly.

Heating Foods

Using methods such as either by using the microwave, stove top, convection ovens, or double boilers are a permitted way to properly heat foods. When heating the hot food items always bring to the internal temperature of (165°F) for 15 seconds. When storing heated foods on hot station the temperature should be maintained at (135°F) or higher.

If the temperature drops below (135°F) then you need to reheat the item back up to (165°F) for 15 seconds. Stir the food and take the temperature of the foods every 2 hours to ensure proper time and temperature. Serving safe foods are everyone's responsibility.

Kitchen Training
Safe Minimum Cooking Temperatures

Category	Food	Temperature	Rest Time
Ground Meat & Meat Mixtures	Beef, Pork, Veal, Lamb	160°F	None
	Turkey, Chicken	165°F	None
Fresh Beef, Veal, Lamb	Steaks, roasts, chops	145°F	3 minutes
Poultry	Chicken & Turkey, whole	165°F	None
	Poultry breasts, roasts	165°F	None
	Poultry thighs, legs, wings	165°F	None
	Duck & Goose	165°F	None
	Stuffing (cooked alone or in bird)	165°F	None
Pork and Ham	Fresh pork	145°F	3 Minutes
	Fresh ham (raw)	145°F	3 Minutes
	Precooked ham (to reheat)	140°F	None
Eggs & Egg Dishes	Eggs	Cook until yolk and white are firm	None
	Egg Dishes	160°F	None
Leftovers & Casseroles	Leftovers	165°F	None
	Casseroles	165°F	None
Seafood	Fin Fish	145 or cook until flesh is opaque and separates easily with a fork.	None
	Shrimp, lobster, and crabs	Cook until flesh is pearly and opaque.	None
	Clams, oysters, and mussels	Cook until shells open during cooking.	None
	Scallops	Cook until flesh is milky white or opaque and firm.	None

Steaks & Roasts		
Doneness	Remove from Grill at this Temperature	Final Cooked Temperature
Rare	30 to 135°F	130 to 140°F
Medium rare	140°F	145°F
Medium	155°F	160°F
Well done	165°F	170°F

Kitchen Training
Prep Cook

The Prep Cook Training best practice is for the manager first thing in the morning prior to the prep cook arriving to work is to fill out the prep sheet for the employee. This will save time and money The very first thing the prep cook should do is sanitize all work tables and utensils.

The second thing is to set up a sanitation bucket with clean sanitation water in it. Use test strips to measure the correct amount of sanitation in the water.

Quat Sanitizer: The test strip should read between PPM (150-400 Parts per Million) Normally 220 PPM.

Chlorine Tablets (50 PPM). Utilize the color coding chart in order to determine if the PPM is correct. Match up the number to the color.

Set up the following prior prepping foods:

- Plastic spatulas, ladles, scoops, tongs, mixing bowls and knives
- Measuring devices: measuring cups, measuring spoons, portion bags, portion containers, cutting boards and scales.
- Food approved storage containers and date dots.

Prep cooks are responsible for the rotation of all products – every time they are in a room they need to rotate foods.

A good rule to practice for a prep person is – only prep what the day calls for. Have all the necessary utensils, bowls, measuring cups ready to go.

Prep only one item at a time and when you are done, clean and sanitize the area. Then move on to the next prep item on the prep list.

Also, as they are prepping food items, proper day dots need to be used consistently as they are putting away the food, that's were first in first out (FIFO) comes in.

The manager on duty should peak into the rooms to verify all prep was done and that all foods were properly rotated and date dotted.

The Managers responsibility is checking out all employees.

How to wash your hands properly

Begin by turning on the water to temperature of 110°F. Lather your hands with soap and scrub vigorously up to your elbows for 20 seconds. Rinse with water and dry your hands with a 1ply paper towel. Use a clean 1 ply paper towel to turn off the water.

Hand washing and gloves

It is very important to follow sanitation practices 24/7. You need to wash your hands frequently.

In-fact, washing your hands every time you:

Changing Gloves:

- Change gloves after each prep job. Chang gloves when touching raw foods. Change gloves within 4 hours. Change gloves when they start to tear.
- After you use the restroom. Always remove your apron prior to using the restroom.
- Wash your hands and change your gloves when you touch your hair, face, dirty apron etc.
- After any cleaning task
- After doing a trash run.

Ensure that all hands are washed properly and consistently before touching food in any way.

Give special attention to washing hands before and after handling raw foods as these are particularly potent carriers of bacteria.

Personal Hygiene

Keep clothes, hair, and other personal items away from all food preparation areas. Take extra care when coping with personal illness. Germs from sneezing and coughing are easily transferred by air as well as by hand.

What is the Difference Between Clean and Sanitize?

Cleaning
Removing visible dirt from equipment

Sanitizing
Treating equipment with chemical agents to prevent bacterial contamination.

First clean your containers by removing any dirt, manufacturing dust, oil or residue from previous batches your equipment. Use a good unscented winemaking cleaner, such as Straight or One-Step.

Do not use household cleaners because many of them contain high levels of industrial perfumes, which sink into equipment and stay, effectively contaminating plastic and even glass.

Once the equipment is clean and very well rinsed with clean water, you can sanitize it with a potassium metabisulphite solution: sluice or spray each piece of equipment and either let it drip completely dry or rinse it with clean water.

A good trick is to put your sanitizing solution in a brand-new trigger-spray bottle. A couple of quick squeezes and you've conveniently and easily coated even large or unwieldy objects in sanitizing solution. If you keep the container of sanitation solution tightly sealed, it will last for a month or two at room temperature before you have to make a fresh batch.

Clean Between Jobs

- Use hot, soapy water to clean all supplies, equipment, utensils, and surfaces between food preparation tasks.
- Avoid using the same dish or utensil to handle both raw and cooked foods.

Sanitize Properly
Sanitization provides an extra defense against the transfer of germs and allergens.

It is highly recommended for restaurants and bars to use either:

- **Quat Sanitation**, the strip should read between PPM (150-400 Parts per Million) Normally 220 PPM.
- **Chlorine Tablets** (50 PPM). Utilize the color coding chart in order to determine if the PPM is correct. Match up the number to the color.

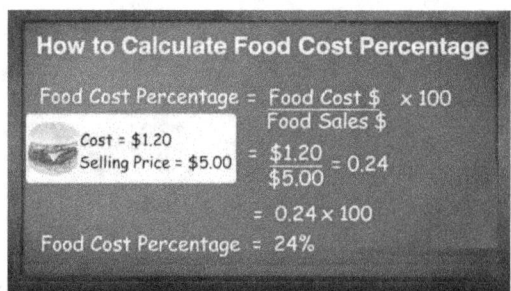

Example, Prairie Ridge Premium Beef Patties (10 lbs., 40 count) for $ 29.71 a case, .74 cents a burger.

The average weight of a head of lettuce was 16.75 ounces per head (just a touch over one pound each). At 89¢ per head, the actual cost per pound was $848.00.

On average, a head of lettuce weighs about 800 grams. Each leaf on a head of lettuce weighs between 6 and 12 ounces. The length and width of each lettuce leaf range from 2 to 3 centimeters

Lettuce on a burger average 28 grams = 0.99 ounces

An average medium-sized tomato weighs 5 to 6 ounces. A small tomato weighs 3 or 4 ounces, and a large tomato weighs 7 ounces or more.

Small tomato (5) tomatoes per pound. Medium tomato (3) tomatoes per pound. Large tomatoes (2) tomatoes per pound.

Let's say, we use 1 large tomato and slice it into 8 slices. Large tomatoes cost $1.69 a pound.

$1.69 divided by 8 slices = 21¢ for each tomato slice.

A medium-sized onion weighs approximately 0.5 pounds or 8 ounces. Go to your local store, look at a bag of onion, and count how many are in the bag. And also write it down and the cost of it, say if a bag of onions cost $2.40 and there are six onions in it, in your calculator put $2.40 in and then divide it by 6, the price of one onion would be 40¢. If you cut the onion in half, then half of the onion would cost 20¢ and so on. Take the cost of the onion 40¢ and divided by 8 slices = 5¢ per slice.

On an average a 28 oz. bottle of ketchup cost $2.06. 3/16 ounces of ketchup on per burger. 128 portions of ketchup per 28 oz. bottle. $2.06 divided by 128 = 16¢.

24 count of American cheese cost an average of $3.74. $3.74 divided by 24 = 16 cents per slice.

Kitchen Training
Food & Drink Menu Costing Procedures

Menu Costing Tool

Use the recipe costing too to cost out your entire menu. List all the ingredients, see the above example. I have included the recipe costing tool system in the restaurant forms and checklist folder located on your computer's desktop.

Last Updated	05/04/17

Menu Item	Hamburger

Ingredients	Recipe Unit	Qty	Unit Cost	Ext Cost
Burger	Each	1.00	$.074	$.074
Bun	Each	1.00	$0.12	$0.12
Cheese	Each	1.00	$0.16	$0.16
Lettuce	Ounce	1.00	$0.15	$0.15
Tomato	Ounce	1.00	$0.08	$0.08
Onion	Ounce	1.00	$0.05	$0.05
Ketchup	Ounce	1.00	$0.02	$0.02
Mustard	Ounce	1.00	$0.02	$0.02
Actual Plate Cost				$1.33
Actual Menu Cost				$5.50
Actual Gross Profit				$4.17
Actual Food Cost %				24.22%
Adjusted Menu Price				$5.67
Adjusted Food Cost %				23.50%
Adjusted Gross Profit				$4.34

For the actual menu costing spreadsheet tool visit:
http://www.workplacewizards.com/?s=Food+costing+tool